MIMESIS
INTERNATIONAL

SOCIOLOGY

n. 4

C000140580

SERGIO BOLOGNA

THE RISE OF THE EUROPEAN SELF-EMPLOYED WORKFORCE

MIMESIS
INTERNATIONAL

Isbn: 9788869770647
Book series: *Sociology*, n. 4

© MIM Edizioni Srl
P.I. C.F. 02419370305

SUMMARY

INTRODUCTION 7

FOR AN ANTHROPOLOGY OF THE SELF-EMPLOYED
WORKER (1997) 15

TEN PARAMETERS FOR DEFINING
A SELF-EMPLOYED WORKERS STATUTE (1997) 101

FROM GENTLEMEN TO MERCENARIES (2011)
THE IDEOLOGY OF PROFESSIONALISM AND ITS CRISIS 149

ACTA, THE FREELANCERS' ASSOCIATION
MANIFESTO OF SECOND GENERATION
SELF-EMPLOYED WORKERS (2010) 223

ORGANIZING THE SELF-EMPLOYED:
A BATTLE FOR SOCIAL JUSTICE (2017) 255

INTRODUCTION

There are different ways to read these essays, which were written over the course of the last 20 years with the specific intention of creating a cultural identity of freelancers in the digital era, those that we call "second-generation independent workers". A simpler and perhaps also the most appropriate way to understand the sense of them is to read these texts as the documentation of a historical process that began in the 1920s and has not yet been completed. The simple fact of calling them second-generation independent workers indicates a particular choice, because we automatically ask ourselves, "Who were the first generation?". The answer can be found in the writings of sociologists and economists, mostly German and Austrian, who studied the social composition and cultural characteristics of independent workers in Europe in the 1920s and 30s, with an eye to the situation in the United States, the country where many of them emigrated to escape the Nazi dictatorship. The essay, "For an Anthropology of the Self-employed Worker", confronts this history.

I imagine that today's Western European or North American independent workers would be unlikely to know that their condition as freelancers had been studied with so much attention in a period when the assembly line had only recently been introduced into mass production. Today's independent workers look to the future, not to the past, and are convinced that they are the new work force. To them, it seems to be a waste of time to take a look back. On the contrary, I believe that they have something to learn, in order to understand themselves better, from the way they have been classified and analysed as independent workers by some of the greatest minds of European sociology such as Emil Lederer, who was a Socialist, and Theodor Geiger, who was a Catholic.

Lederer would become a much appreciated teacher at the New School of Social Research in New York, while Geiger preferred to emigrate to Denmark where he continued his studies on those we today call "knowledge workers", a term that was coined by Paul Drucker and came into common usage in the 1950s. Austrian-born Drucker emigrated to the United States in 1939 and, after WWII, became one of the most important management consulting theoreticians, understanding very early on that the technological development inside big corporations — including the most sophisticated marketing techniques, human resource management, and organisations with complex systems — require specific competences. Drucker understood that a major market of knowledge workers, professionals who were a highly dynamic component of the middle class, was opening up, and that they could carry out their activities either as salaried employees of big companies or as freelancers, second-generation independent workers.

In my work life, I have taught the history of the workers' movement and of the industrial society in various universities in Italy and Germany, but I have also worked for a rather long period as a consultant to governmental institutions, big companies, entrepreneurial associations, and trade unions. I have been a civil servant and an independent professional, a salaried employee and a freelancer. So I have observed that different positions in the labour market, salaried or freelance, have a strong influence on the subjectivity of people and their perception of the world. In the essay, "Ten Parameters for Defining a Self-employed Workers Statute", I have tried to define the difference between those who work for themselves and those who work as employees. A difference in terms of what? In terms of their perception of space and time, regarding management of their competences, regarding their perception of earning and remuneration (wage vs. invoice), but also the difference regarding a citizen's right to health care and a pension — a particularly strong difference between Europe's welfare model and that of the United States.

Reasoning in these terms, and especially on the problem of "human capital" that every conscientious worker possesses and that represents his vital heritage, I understood that it was necessary to face the problem of professionalism. What is a profession? Who is a professional? Is management consulting a profession? Or is a profession just a competence acquired with a precise study curriculum? I studied theology, literature, history and philosophy. Management consultants are usually economists, engineers and lawyers. Do I have the right to call myself a professional? The first to confront the problem of "profession" was Max Weber, but he spoke about the profession of teaching, so he was really talking about a mission, a vocation (*Beruf*), and not about the performance of a service in a business operation. This was handled by sociologists specialising in professions. I took a close look at their analyses in the essay, "From Gentlemen to Mercenaries", written in 2010, at the same time that we of ACTA were determining our program and writing our manifesto (see below).

However, as I said above, what motivated me to write these essays was not academic interest. It was not my intention to acquire titles in order to apply for some university position. I have dealt with history, not sociology, and in particular the history of workers' organisations, the history of the cultures and ideologies that have made the formation of trade unions possible, the history of protest movements, of strikes, the story of *Arbeiterräte* in Germany and of the Wobblies in the United States.

This interest of mine for the history of trade union movements was also driven by my militant and activist activities in the radical movements of the 1960s and 70s, in support of the wildcat strikes of Fiat workers and French students who occupied the Sorbonne in May 1968. So when I began to think about my professional freelance consulting experience, I asked myself: Is there an association, a trade union, that represents independent workers per se, the new

10

professionals who work with the Internet, the creative workers, those who perform services in companies and institutions as freelancers? Taking a good look around me, I could quickly verify that that there were many guilds, many associations for single professions, but there was no association or trade union for independent workers per se, one that covers all professions. There were associations for translators or web designers, film directors or logistics consultants, but there was no association that represented all of them: a freelance trade union. It seemed to me that a cultural background that could form — or contribute to forming — a social identity, a class identity, was missing. It was the limited consciousness of their own social identity that impeded the birth of an all-inclusive representative organisation of the professions.

I wrote these essays in the hope of contributing to the creation of this consciousness. Fortunately and to my great surprise, when the two essays, "Ten Parameters for Defining a Self-employed Workers Statute" and "For an Anthropology of Self-employed Workers", were published in 1997 by the Italian publishing house, Feltrinelli, a public debate developed. It was not so much provoked by my supporters, of whom there were relatively few, but by my critics, including some of the most important sociological and economic experts on Italian labour, who contested my definition of second-generation independent workers. On the other hand, labour law professors were very intrigued. Still, while a part of the academic culture continued to be conservative, my proposals were discussed and

11

recognised as valid and pertinent by a group of workers in Milan who were discussing among themeselves the opportunity to create an association. They were also encouraged by the experience of the Freelancers Union in the United States, which was established in the same period in which I was writing my essays.

In 2004, ACTA, was founded; originally called "Associazione Consulenti del Terziario Avanzato" (Association of Advanced Tertiary Consultants), the name was later changed to "ACTA, the Freelancers Association". I became a member and a board member and contributed to drafting its Manifesto, which is partially translated here.

ACTA went on to become one of the first members of the European Forum of Independent Professionals (EFIP), of which it has assumed the Vice-Presidency. For many years, it was ignored by politicians, governments and other associations, but in the end it finally succeeded in "breaking through", to become a privileged representative to the Ministry of Labour and to the Presidency of the Council of Ministers. Their efforts led to the approval of some important reforms: the reform of obligatory contributions to public pensions; approval of the Statute of Independent Work that offers some fiscal advantages and recognition of some important civil rights for independent workers. In May 2017, on the 20th anniversary of the publication of my essays, at a congress held at the Ca' Foscari University of Venice, in which Sara Horowitz, founder of the U.S-based Freelancers Union, also participated, I was given the opportunity to assess the results of this experience. A slightly modified version of my talk is included here with the title, "Organising the Self-Employed: A Battle for Social Justice".

Sergio Bologna
Translation by Kristy Lynn Davis

FOR AN ANTHROPOLOGY
OF THE SELF-EMPLOYED WORKER

"Yeah, he's self-unemployed"
(from the film *Palookaville*, 1996)

In his last published book (September 1996), one of Europe's leading experts on the subject of self-employment offered his readers a brief but intense reconstruction of empirical studies and theoretical reflections conducted in Germany and Austria by sociologists, economists and statisticians in the first three decades of the 20th century.[1] The subjects of these studies were transformations of the production model, the emergence of the large organised enterprise according to Taylor's scientific management systems, and their effects on social structures. The phenomena observed by these researchers were chiefly marked by a rapid influx of labour from the area of self-employment to the large enterprise system. Due to its vast scope and long-term consequences, it seemed to be a phenomenon similar to that of the *enclosures* in England when, following a number of measures that banned the collective use of land, a mass of proletarians were obliged to "sell"

---

1   Dieter Bögenhold, *Das Dienstleistungsjahrhundert. Kontinuitäten und Diskontinuitäten in Wirtschaft und Gesellschaft* (Stuttgart: Enke Verlag, 1996).

themselves in the new labour market created by the first industrial revolution, without any bargaining power.

In 1907 Werner Sombart published the first survey on individual enterprises (*Alleinbetriebe*), and in 1912 Emil Lederer's degree thesis on clerical workers was published. In the same year, Schumpeter published his *Theory of Economic Development*. During the time of the Weimar republic, the study of the middle classes and of self-employment, or "new" self-employment, naturally intensified, with an the emergence of an unexpected phenomenon that went against early-century predictions. Despite the expansion of large factories, the percentage of enterprises employing fewer than ten employees remained above 90% of all enterprises throughout the duration of the republic (1918–1933). A number of researches and reflections that remain topical were then carried out by sociologists such as Götz Briefs, and by the most clear-sighted of all, Theodor Geiger, who in 1928 published a study on the social relevance of self-employed workers after having carefully analysed industrial censuses.[2]

---

2 When the Nazis came to power (1933) numerous sociologists emigrated to the United States, where some of their writings were translated for a small group of specialists and students at Columbia University and the New School for Social Research in New York. Mariuccia Salvati has obtained these texts and translated some of them into Italian, adding an important introductory essay, *Da Berlino a New York. Crisi della classe media e futuro della democrazia nelle scienze sociali degli Anni Trenta* (Bologna: Cappelli, 1989).

Taking up this line of thought, I read or, in a few cases, re-read the most important texts of these German sociologists written before the advent of Nazism.[3]

The shift from the age of self-employment to that of salaried work in the writings of Emil Lederer, 1912–1914

If one considers that the biggest contribution made by these scholars came in the area of modernisation and related phenomena resulting from a change in the productive paradigm, then the central figure during that period of sociological thought was Emil Lederer. He was the first to have appreciated the quantum shift happening with the progressive spread of salaried employment to the detriment of the area of self-employment. Notes drafted in 1913 and resumed in 1919, entitled "The society of non-independent workers. Psycho-social habitus of the present", illustrate the basic traits of this historical shift, governed by the Taylorist system.[4] Empirical materials

---

3   In addition to the single works of various authors, cited individually, I reviewed the years from 1918 to 1933 of the "Archiv für Sozialwissenschaft und Sozialpolitik", (ASS) founded by Werner Sombart, Max Weber and Edgar Jaffe in concert with Joseph Schumpeter and Alfred Weber, published by Emil Lederer and the annals of the journal "Die Arbeit".

4   Emil Lederer, *Die Gesellschaft der Unselbständigen. Zum sozialpsychischen Habitus der Gegenwart*, in *Kapitalismus, Klassenstruktur und Probleme der*

supplied by industrial censuses had already shown that the Taylorist system had been widely adopted in German factories. Lederer was not interested in understanding its consequences in terms of income distribution, but rather its anthropological impact, in order to understand the *seelische Verfassung* (frame of mind), *geistige Physiognomie* (spiritual traits), and *kulturelle Attitüde* (cultural attitude), in short the *change of mindset* caused by the shifting of the workforce from the state of *wirtschaftlich Berufstätige* to that of *unselbständig Berufstätige* (from independent to salaried). Lederer noted that the problem stemmed from the fact that observers had not changed their mindset, and continued to think with the mind of the previous century, believing that the labour force could be commanded freely and independently. It was difficult to understand the mentality of the employee when the observer enjoyed an independent status.

One of the biggest differences between the mentality of the old-style independent worker and that of the Taylorist non-independent worker, Lederer believed, was the "periodisation" of life.

For one, life is a continuum enclosed within a family unit, where the unit of time is life itself, and the unit of

Demokratie in Deutschland 1910–1940, Ausgewählte Aufsätze mit einem Beitrag von Hans Speier und einer Bibliographie von Bernd Uhlmannsieck, ed. by J. Kocka (Göttingen: Vandenhoeck § Ruprecht, 1979), pp. 14–32. The same volume contains the essay on Taylorism, equally important for our subject, Emil Lederer, *Die ökonomische und soziale Bedeutung des Taylorsystems*, pp. 83–96.

space is the family; for the other (the example given is that of a civil servant), life is marked by a privilege that cannot be passed on to one's family and by an income scale (salary increments) that represents one's entire economic potential. Private sector employees are different. For them, economic existence is dependent not on the possession of means of production but on the signature of an employment contract. Unlike the civil servant, however, their economic existence is based not only on a single period of work, but on several work periods in different companies. And for the factory worker, periods of work alternating with periods of non-work, reduced job security, the seasonal nature of work and economic crises lead him to an existence based on even shorter units of time. As the basis of one's life moves away from stability and veers towards job insecurity, personal relations — the system of relations with other persons — become ever more important, yet also more unstable. "The essence of such a shift is that life (from an economic point of view) loses both stability and continuity."[5] Lederer's consideration relates to the classic process of alienation, in which the person and his actions are no longer one and the same, but actions, represented by work procedures and obligations, are anonymous. As changes arrive more quickly and the unit of time of guaranteed economic existence gets shorter, people come to have a changing relationship with things, an internalisation of the provisional as a normal time

5   Emil Lederer, *Die ökonomische und...*, p. 18.

mode. The major events of life are not etched in a family chronology, acquiring relevance and meaning, but exist in and of themselves, without an underlying context, forming a totality for the person concerned but almost hanging in the air (*freischwebend*), a totality devoid of a centre of attraction or a backdrop.

Lederer hones in on the problem of the individual's atomisation, of his being interchangeable in respect of work performed, and raises the question of whether or not the collectivisation of the means of production proposed by socialism can be successful — seeing that Taylorism has separated man not only from the means of production but also from individually characterised work, creating an atomised mass of existences that are unable to govern themselves, as they are unable to repossess the working sequence. He gives a negative answer to this question, arguing that the collective ownership of means of production would in any case continue a non-personalised relationship between the worker and the means of production, thus it would not cause changes to the individual's "frame of mind" and would not change man and his points of reference towards others. For this reason, the anarchic ideal, in which both the relationship between the producer and the means of production and between the producer and requirements are a direct, personal, concrete and contextual relationship, appeared to him to be more suitable for taking mankind outside the atomisation of non-independence, compared with the socialist ideal of collectivisation. The prospect of self-management, however, appeared to him to be historically further

20

away than the prospective duration of the capitalistic society, for which reason it is useful for "lowering the target" and reflecting on possible forms of social security, which can to an extent provide an element of stability to non-independent workers. Whereas the forms of insurance of self-employed workers are aimed at protecting against the loss of the means of production in their possession (land for the farmer, shop and goods in the storeroom for the trader, horse and cart for the coachman), in terms of value or damage, the form of insurance for the employee is that which allows him to counter the precarious nature of the employment relationship (the risk of unemployment, guaranteed old-age pension, etc.) in terms of continuity, and thus to re-establish, through state intervention, a life-long security that approaches that of civil servants or self-employed workers.

We must not forget, of course, that Lederer was writing at a time when the open-ended labour contract was common only among civil servants. In the private sector, workers were not yet afforded employment protection, and the independent existence envisaged by Lederer was that of the "old style" self-employed worker whose independence was based on ownership of the means required to generate income.

The image of the self-employed worker that possesses only his labour and his skill is a long way from Lederer's perspective, yet if one puts his examples into historical context, we believe it is important to remember that the problem of an anthropological change, a radical change in the collective mentality as

21

a result of a change in the productive paradigm, had been raised very clearly when Taylorism and Fordism first came into being.

Lederer's teachings encourage us to follow the approach adopted by him to characterise the transition process from independence to non-independence, and to transfer it, naturally not to the letter, to the modern day when, with Post-Fordism, the reverse process took place.

Lederer tried to test his hypotheses on the change in mindset with white-collar workers, studying their growth in the Wilhelminian period, focusing on clerical workers in the private sector. The 1912 essay on white-collar workers, *Die Angestellten im Wilhelminischen Reich,* knowingly stayed away from the *communis opinio* of "orthodox" Marxism and its schematics. Not only did he refuse to include white-collar workers among the proletariat or the new middle classes, he refused to consider them as a uniform group, such as to form a single "community of interests" (or pressure group).[6] Following on from the example of engineers in private industry and also of a part of the commercial staff in large companies, he argued that there remained a great deal of tension between being non-independent, performing salaried work in a business organisation, and being independent, free to organise one's own work and freed from the obligations of Taylorism. White-

---

6   Emil Lederer, *Die Angestellten im Wilhelminischen Reich*, in *Kapitalismus, Klassenstruktur...*, pp. 51–82.

collar workers seemed to him to be the main form of transition from traditional self-employment to subordinate employment. Over 48% of white-collar workers in the late-Wilhelminian era came from families of self-employed workers of all kinds; 30% came from self-employed workers whose activities were connected with the production of goods. The hypothesis was that a shift was going on within social strata that had a middle-class mentality. In short, Lederer rejected the idea of a progressive political integration between blue-collar and white-collar workers, and also the idea that white-collar workers might represent the "new middle classes". Rather, they appeared destined to remain suspended in an area "between the classes". The biggest problem was not that of knowing whether this class of worker would shift towards conservative or progressive positions, but rather that of understanding that the spread of salaried employment was creating a generation that had a new way of thinking and a new mindset.

In 1920 Lederer resumed his documented analysis of the development of white-collar workers. Shocked by the expulsion of engineers and office clerks during the course of the "rationalisation", he would focus on phenomena relating to technological unemployment, publishing in 1931 a masterly essay on that subject.[7]

---

7   Emil Lederer, *Technischer Fortschritt und Arbeitslosigkeit* (Tübingen: Mohr, 1931).

Theodor Geiger and the sociographic method

About twenty years elapsed from the writings of Lederer to Theodor Geiger's work, *Die soziale Schichtung des deutschen Volkes*, during the course of which occurred the tragedy of the Great War and the democratic experience of the Weimar republic, Hyperinflation, and the Great Depression. The nature of the Taylorist-Fordist system had been laid bare, and the analysis of self-employment issues had taken stock of these profound experiences. Geiger had studied very topical issues and followed the phenomena of modernisation not only in terms of capitalism but also with regard to what we now term the "voluntary sector". He had studied the phenomena of advertising and open universities and felt the need to bring his "sociographic" studies into a sort of conceptual framework.

The book written in 1932 and discussed here was intended as a sociographic study.[8] But what exactly did Geiger mean by sociography? It is a method for describing differences within the social fabric, done by cross-referencing data and analyses on lifestyles, mental and cultural traits with data and analyses on economic conditions and professional positions. Economic sociology looks at how given mentalities

---

8   Theodor Geiger, *Die soziale Schichtung des deutschen Volkes. Soziographisches Versuch auf statistischer Grundlage*, facsimile of the first edition (1932) published by Enke Verlag, Stuttgart 1987.

can be the driving forces of economic development and can thus lead to the formation of social blocks, or socioeconomic strata (*Schichten*). Sociography seeks to break down the various *Schichtmentalitäten* — the ways of thinking typical of a social stratum — so as to identify various "blocks" of the social body according to their "mindset" and to their role in the social division of labour.

Geiger's concept of *Schicht* thus has a cultural basis, while the roots of *Klasse* lie in production relations. *Schicht* is taken to mean an affinity of style (*Stilverwandschaft*), a frame of mind, and is a concept that is inextricably linked to that of social movements.[9]

Geiger believed that neither the social strata nor social classes, but only the specific and respective areas of recruitment, were "quantifiable". Social statistics (*Sozialstatistik*) thus have the important task of supporting political sociology, helping to define in quantitative terms the potential basis of mindsets of the various professional groups and the virtual recipients of political ideologies.

In order to attain a high degree of differentiation and identification of specific social traits, sociography makes use of small sample analyses, of "case studies" conducted on individual professionals, broken down by place of residence, age, gender, electoral behaviour and so on. The sample survey reveals the mindsets

---

9   Theodor Geiger, 'Zur Theorie des Klassenbegriffs und der proletarischen Klasse', *Schmollers Jahrbuch*, 54 (Berlin 1930), 185–236.

and any differences in mentalities within the same professional group. Statistics must, therefore, have the same degree of differentiation as the sociographic analysis, proceeding by ever greater degrees of disaggregation (*Tiefgliederung*).

The starting point for Geiger's analysis is the census of trades and professions conducted in 1925. These data were supplemented by information from business censuses collected in 1924 and 1928, the survey on crafts in 1930, and annual statistics on income taxes and the population.

The first approximate breakdown (*Rohgliederung*) consisted of three sectors: the upper sector (or stratum) (*Oberschicht*), corresponding to the status of "capitalist"; the medium sector (*Mittelschicht*), corresponding to the status of "middle class"; and the lower sector (*Unterschicht*), corresponding to the status of "proletarian". The various social blocks and professional stratifications can be distributed among the three sectors, without being confined to any one sector. Some self-employed workers can be classified, by virtue of their revenue and mindset, into *Oberschicht* alongside "capitalists".

Rebellion against the schematics of the Marxist vulgate

In this classification, Geiger makes increasing use in his treatise of the term *Lage*, making the distinction between high, medium and low status, since this classification is obtained from quantifiable information (individual income, size of enterprise, size of farmland, etc.) and, as such, is statistically measurable. As already mentioned, the term *Schicht* refers to cultural and behavioural paradigms, to mindsets and, as such, are unquantifiable criteria. It is, however, preferable to the term *Stand*, in relation to which Geiger remained suspicious, wondering how useful it was to carry on talking about *Mittelstand*, a term commonly used for "middle class", also to be found in the definition of small and medium enterprises (*mittelständisches Unternehmen*), without this leading to some confusion. Geiger argued that the term *Stand* has a cultural meaning, referring to the historical period prior to the bourgeois revolutions, when *Stände* stood for the privileged classes, the castes holding the reins of power, and the professional guilds (e.g. *kaufmännische Stände*). The term continues to be used in the contemporary era, again with reference to a social status that enjoys special privileges, a legal status that is different from others, such as civil servants (*Beamtenstand*). The modern middle classes, both "old" and "new" (*alter und neuer Mittelstand*), are marked by their being formed through social, economic and cultural processes undergoing continual change, and through social mobility processes moving people upwards and downwards.

Rejecting the ontological value of the term *Klasse*, *Stand* and *Schicht*, and reducing them to simple tools of sociographic analysis, Geiger appears to emerge as the theoretician-practitioner of "galaxy-type" social formations.[10]

Geiger acknowledges his debt to Gustav Schmoller, Werner Sombart and Max Weber for preparing the method for his conceptual framework. Although there were keen differences between them, they were united by their efforts to move beyond the powerful schematics of the Marxist vulgate, which entails the division of society into two basic classes, the proletariat and the bourgeoisie, given as the result of the raging growth of industrialism and the capitalistic production method, tearing asunder what remained of the "intermediate" classes, relegating them to the detritus of pre-capitalism. Sombart and Weber's reaction, as interpreted by Geiger in the initial part of *Die soziale Schichtung des deutschen Volkes*, was aimed at contextualising the social, historical and economic foundations of the concept of class, defining it as a cultural artefact, the product of an ideology and of cultural/behavioural stratifications. Adding his name to this school of thought, Geiger sought to

---

10 Theodor Geiger, 'Die Gruppe und die Kategorien Gemeinschaft und Gesellschaft', *ASS*, 58 (Leipzig, 1927), 338–374; he would take up the question of "group" category the following year with 'Gruppe als verwirklichtes Ich-Ideal', *Archiv für angewandte Soziologie*, I, nos. 2/3 (Berlin, 1928), pp. 23 et seq.; the greater the analytical relevance of the "group" category the more the structure of society is akin to a "galaxy" arranged on different layers.

make a contribution to post-Marxist sociology and demonstrate that:

1) from a statistical point of view, the predicted disappearance of the so-called "intermediate" strata and their integration into the two basic classes had not happened

2) from a sociological point of view, instead of fading away, the so-called "intermediate" strata showed a capacity to resist and transform internally that re-placed them at the centre of the story

3) in terms of empirical research there were so many differences within the two (or three) basic classes that they could not be considered as homogenous aggregates but as "galaxies"

4) the social condition of the blue-collar worker, determined by his role in the production process, did not necessarily produce growth in his "class conscience"; however, thanks to the possibility of social mobility, workers could become "bourgeois" during economic upswings, when there was a dearth of labour and stable wages, or be stripped of their class "upgrade" during economic crises and periods of long-term unemployment when workers were dragged down to the level of "underclass".

Geiger's "sociographic" manifesto appears to be that of objecting to the historical determinism of the inevitable division of society into just two classes, underlining the role of the "new" intermediate classes, challenging the internal uniformity of the three basic classes, and stressing the importance of upward and downward social mobility. It is thus clear why Geiger should be interested in the *Selbständige*, self-employed workers.

The reaction to the Marxist vulgate came not only from areas opposed to socialism, it found supporters among liberal and catholic sociologists, such as Götz Briefs, and was particularly popular among scholars engaged in radical- or anarchic-oriented civil battles, such as Lederer, Kracauer and Speier, who in many ways may appear to be harbingers of the "new left" of the 1960s and 1970s, being linked to more recent movements by the search for innovation in political thought and by social analysis, the rejection of dogmas that are oft-repeated and set in stone by a caste of bureaucrats. Geiger himself did not reject the concept of class conscience, he refuted the idea that this was a necessary consequence of a social condition and that it was sufficient to ascertain the role of a social group in the production relationship in order to understand the dominant mentality. Bearing in mind Mannheim's teaching, Geiger believed that class conscience was a product of ideology and not a mentality typical of salaried workers, was pertinent to the sphere of politics and organisation, and was not a frame of mind. He preferred to talk about *proletarische Lage*, the "condition of proletarian", rather than "proletariat". He fought hard against the hypothesis of "proletarisation" of the middle classes, in particular white-collar workers, always putting forward his sociographic interpretations, which highlighted the complexity of the social fabric, to contrast views that trivialised ongoing changes with predetermined ideological formulas.[11]

The "old" and "new" middle classes

With the evident growth of a new "clerical" middle class and the reduction in the percentage of blue-collar workers among all workers, the approach of social democratic publications had been to merge salaried clerical work with manual work, coining the term *Stehkragenproletarier*, a proletariat of white-collar workers, literally "proletarians with a starched collar". This new clerical class, just as devoid of

---

11   Theodor Geiger, 'Zur Kritik der Verbürgerlichung', *Die Arbeit*, 7 (1931), 534–553; see also 'Die Mittelschichten und die Sozialdemokratie', *Die Arbeit*, 8 (1931), 619–635. Following the electoral success of the NSDAP in the 1930 elections, the question of crisis/proletarisation of the bourgeoisie and crisis/ embourgeoisement of the proletariat was examined by a number of authors in the social democratic press, such as Ernst Wilhelm Eschmann, 'Zur 'Krise' des Bürgertums', *Die Arbeit*, 5 (1931), 362–371; Rudolf Küstermeier, 'Die Proletarisierung des Mittelstandes und die Verwirklichung des Sozialismus', *Die Arbeit*, 10 (1931), 761–774; Max Victor, 'Verbürgerlichung des Proletariats und Proletarisierung des Mittelstandes. Eine Analyse der Einkommenschichtung nach dem Kriege', *Die Arbeit*, 1 (1931), 17–31; Svend Riemer, 'Mittelstand und sozialistische Politik', *Die Arbeit*, 5 (1932), 265–272.

means of production as the working class and under the orders and control of the enterprise, would soon abandon its "false conscience" and recognise its community of interests with factory workers, giving rise to a single front in favour of socialism. Further to the sociological studies conducted on the white-collar clerical class, Geiger rejected this division, and tackled "sociographic" problems in accordance with the following logical sequence:

1) the first distinction to be made whenever one examines those social classes that do not fit into the two basic categories of capitalists and blue-collar workers is that regarding the criteria for defining the "old" and the "new" middle classes, or first- and second-generation middle classes, the former to be found in the pre-capitalist set-up and the latter in the modern capitalism of the large factories

2) the core of the "old" middle classes was made up of farmers, craftsmen and small traders, in other words basically self-employed workers. The core of the "new" middle classes was made up of white-collar workers, partly from the liberal professions and partly from the "new" civil service, risen from the modernisation of the state and its functions (welfare state, administrative decentralisation, and so on) in the shift from the old monarchic system to the new Weimar democracy

3) whereas the clerical class was the biggest component of the "new middle classes", it had to

be stressed that within this clerical class — as the studies of Lederer and Kracauer had highlighted and as had another important sociologist of the period, Tobis — there were so many differences to suggest that the new middle classes were in actual fact a *galaxy* made up of many different figures, with different and sometimes opposing mindsets. One such example was the difference between production and control engineers of the large Taylorist company and civil servants (*Beamten*).[12]

4) faced with such a complex situation, the question was asked whether the concept of *Mittelstand*, the middle class, was actually a "non-concept" (*Unbegriff*), and whether it might be preferable to adopt a set of new more apt concepts for the various configurations of the social strata. This

---

12   For a discussion on the social status of employees, I refer again to the anthology edited by Mariuccia Salvati (see note 2) and to the prefaces of the Italian editions of Kracauer's book, *Gli Impiegati*, ed. by Luciano Gallino (Turin: Einaudi, 1980), and Jürgen Kocka's book, *Impiegati tra fascismo e democrazia. Una storia sociale-politica degli impiegati: America e Germania (1890–1940)* (Naples: Liguori Editore, 1982). Tobis had taken part in the crafts survey (1930) and had studied the question of white-collar workers; see *Die wirtschaftliche und soziale Lage der Angestellten* (Berlin, 1931). One of the first contributions, apart from Lederer's works, came from Fritz Croner, *Die Angestelltenbewegung nach der Währungsstabilisierung*, *ASS*, 60, 1, 103–146, partly translated in the anthology edited by Mariuccia Salvati.

also applied to self-employed workers, who were statistically more numerous in the lower group, that of the proletarian condition, than might have been imagined. This led to the belief that second-generation self-employed workers, downgraded and impoverished in the Weimar republic, were much different from the first-generation independent workers of the late 19th century, who formed the core of the "old" middle classes.

Based on this logic, Geiger was able to pick up again the analysis of the *Selbständige* in the late Weimar era, but came up against difficulties when trying to place worker categories in one of the broad social strata that had been identified, in particular groups of low-income self-employed workers and "new craftsmen".[13]

The recruitment base for "poor" self-employed workers was above all traditional self-employment: farmers, craftsmen and small traders overwhelmed by the development of industrialism, large factories and urbanisation, who had ended up losing their professional identity completely. The farmer had become a labourer or occasional porter, the craftsman had sought to supplement his income with small trades, opening up the "dual occupation" market (*Nebenberuf*) that Geiger analysed in depth in order to grasp the specific aspects of "poor" self-employment.

A radical transformation had submerged the world of craft enterprises, creating a ruthless choice between

---

13   Theodor Geiger, 'Statistische Analyse der wirtschaftlich Selbständigen', *ASS*, 69 (1933), 407–439.

crisis-hit traditional crafts and "new crafts", taken to mean micro-enterprises supplying services to large companies, based on relations that anticipated by half a century the modern-day network enterprise that makes widespread use of *outsourcing*.[14] According to the

---

14   The analysis of the craft firm is one of the most interesting aspects of Weimarian industrial sociology, the main source being the 1930 survey, which led to Kiel economist Gerhard Colm's assertion that "modern crafts have managed to use all technological inventions (as a driving force) to the extent that they are profitable for the small enterprise. They sought to enhance their products in a competitive market, accepting the challenge of competing with industry. In short, craft enterprises have today taken on the form of small firms.", in *Kapitalistische und nichtkapitalistische Elemente in der heutigen deutschen Volkswirtschaft*, in Various Authors, *Kapitalismus Klassenstruktur und Probleme der Demokratie in Deutschland 1910–1940* (Göttingen, 1979), p. 115. This awareness of the shift from the crafts of medieval origin to modern crafts is also present in Schumpeter, related to his idea of the family as a socio-economic category: "the family, not the physical person, is the true individual in the class theory", in 'Die sozialen Klassen im ethnisch homogenen Milieu', *ASS*, 57 (1927), republished in Joseph Schumpeter, *Aufsätze zur Soziologie* (Tübingen: Mohr, 1953). The "ethnically homogeneous" setting brings to mind the theorising of the 1970s and 80s regarding the sub-cultures of industrial districts, social cohesion as a precondition for the development of innovative small enterprises. Other sociological considerations made by Schumpeter are not so stimulating, for example, the attempt to analyse class stratification in the essay that raised concerns from Geiger, 'Das soziale Antlitz des deutschen Reiches', pp. 214–225,

1930 study on craft firms, the first group was mostly made up of individual enterprises (*Alleinhandwerker* or *Null-Betriebe*) or firms in which the craftsman made use of family help (*mithelfende Familienangehörige*), which Geiger usually placed in the lower group. The second group was made up of small and medium enterprises, having precise functions in the division of labour, but heavily conditioned by large companies, whose owners Geiger placed in the "intermediate" group and, in special cases, in the upper group, that of "capitalists".

Self-employed workers as "proletaroids"

These new situations, constantly altered by short-term events or industrial policies (Hyperinflation, Rationalisation, the Great Depression), required new concepts and new definitions. Geiger took from Sombart and Briefs the term *Proletaroid*, indicating self-employed workers placed in the lower group but distinct from actual proletarians, low-skilled salaried workers in industry, agriculture and services. "From a

---

first published in *Bonner Mitteilungen*, 1 (1929), 3–14; in this essay, Schumpeter completely ruled out the possibility that German voters could be attracted by extremist parties. A year later, in the 1930 elections, the Nazis and Communists made their breakthroughs. In addition to craft firms, retail trade was the subject of studies by government commissions; see Jenny Radt, 'Der Einzelhandel im Licht der Enquetevernehmungen', *Die Arbeit*, 8, 538–545.

legal point of view and in terms of work organisation, the proletaroid is the master of his working life. In other words, he is in charge of supplying his professional services and is not bound by the instructions and orders of a master. This differentiates him from the salaried proletariat. Both types, however, share the position of being under the pressure of demand, in that they are obliged to reproduce their work every day, to enable them to survive. The enterprise lives under the watchful eye of the owner; if that supervision is missing for one or two days, the enterprise will fall apart. He works on his own account, but, just like the salaried worker, he basically survives by virtue of his own labour. From an economic point of view, he receives income for work performed, like the salaried worker. Legally, he is a figure that brings together in the same person the roles of employer and employee."[15] The terms "self-employed" and "independent" may serve to designate a "social block" (*die Selbständige*), but within this block it is necessary to distinguish self-employed workers that are in some way owners of an asset (piece of land, a shop) from self-employed workers that only have their labour to offer. For the latter, in particular those placed in the "proletaroid" group, Geiger uses the term *Tagewerker in eigener Rechnung*, which we might translate as "daily worker working on his own account".

It is interesting to note that Geiger distinguishes the work provided by self-employed workers from

---

15   Theodor Geiger, *Die soziale Schichtung...*, p. 31.

that of occasional salaried workers, for whom the social statistics of the Weimar republic had coined the term *Lohnarbeiter wechselnder Art*, which we might translate as "mobile salaried workers", whose remuneration was based on a unit of time, an hourly rate (even though in many sectors, e.g. transport and handling of goods, occasional workers were paid by the day). Between these two figures, the independent "daily" worker and mobile salaried worker, Geiger inserted a marginal type of figure, that of "homeworkers", making the distinction in this group between those workers who receive the raw material and orders from an intermediary acting on behalf of a large company, thus comparable with the industrial proletariat (*Heimarbeiter*), and workers that purchase the raw materials themselves and send the products to their own customers (*in eigener Regie Hausgewerbe Treibende*).

The term "proletaroid" also covered traits that were not purely economic, but also political. Geiger defined the "proletaroids as that part of the old middle classes or traditional self-employed that have resigned themselves to their progressive economic marginalisation", basically small traders who had opened a store in the early years of the Weimar republic, despite not having any qualification or capital reserve and who, in his opinion, alone made up one seventh of the entire mass of self-employed workers, or former owners of small farms, forced to find parallel employment. Geiger believed these small traders were the least qualified and least dynamic part of the new self-employed of the 1920s, living a "parasite-like existence" if their social and economic function were to be compared with the growth of department stores and consumer cooperatives. He believed they were the reserve of National Socialism (Nazi) votes, as they were inclined to project and sublimate their resignation to their economic marginalisation in visions of national-patriotic palingenesis.

Can analysis of the method adopted by Geiger to "sociographically" describe work help to provide us with some ideas that can be used in today's analysis of self-employment? To a certain degree, yes, and what has been written above appears to give some interesting pointers. What must be stressed is the importance of the distinction between salaried work and self-employment, a fundamental distinction that emerges not so much from Geiger's theoretical considerations and definitions of method as from the content of essays written after the 1932 book, presented to the reader as elaborations and further analyses of the fourth paragraph of the second chapter.

In *Die soziale Schichtung des deutschen Volkes*, Geiger had mentioned five statistically measurable entities: self-employed workers (*Selbständige*), family workers (*mithelfende Familienangehörige*), white-collar workers and officials (*Angestellten und Beamten*), blue-collar workers (*Arbeiter*) and the jobless (*Berufslose*). In the following two essays, he reduced the number of categories to just two: *Arbeitnehmer* (employees or dependent workers) and *Selbständige* (self-employed or independent workers).[16] He warned his readers, however, that these categories were not absolute since, within both the first and second group, some intermediate forms could be found (*Zwischenformen* or *Mischfiguren*) with different mindsets. Geiger gave a somewhat surprising view of the "new middle classes". Far from having an innovative impact on society and producing a new bourgeoisie of high income professions above the average of more skilled workers, he argued the *neuer Mittelstand* had produced a condition of minimum incomes and marginalisation, causing the majority of *Tagewerker in eigener Rechnung und Regie* to increase the number of proletaroids, devoid of a professional identity, class or group culture, forgotten by appeals to a socialism reserved for salaried workers, former blue-collar workers or unemployed employees, or to the productive middle classes (technicians, specialists, exponents of new professions). For this reason, the ears of these "autonomous" proletaroids would hear more keenly the appeals launched by Nazi agitators.

The end result of Geiger's statistical calculations was as follows: the area of self-employment in Germany on the eve of Nazism extended to a little over 20 million people (only about 50% of whom were active), inclusive of all types of self-employed workers (liberal professions, industry, crafts, trade, transport, agriculture and about 3 million family workers). Of these, 41.1%

---

16   Theodor Geiger, 'Soziale Gliederung der deutschen Arbeitnehmer', *ASS*, 69 (1933), 151–188; reference to the second article is given in note 13.

were included in the proletaroid group, 55.9% in the intermediate group, and 3.0% in the capitalist group.

Geiger saw self-employed workers as an inert social block, devoid of dynamism both internally (*stationär*) and in quantitative terms: "The number of independent existences in industry and commerce is static in both relative and absolute terms".[17]

The "grey area" specialist

Should we wish to give a final opinion about Geiger's "sociographic" writings, we may state that the most original and interesting aspects of his research are those that are able to hone in on the "grey area" located on the edges of one period and another, between one method of production and another, highlighting figures with blurred boundaries, such as second occupation workers (*Nebenberuf*), unpaid family workers (*mithelfende Familienangehörige*), individual firms ("an indicator of the condition of proletaroid") or "new" craftsmen. With regard to this, he gave some very lucid definitions that were echoed by other sociologists of the period, a sign that Geiger had perfectly grasped the difference between pre-capitalist crafts, belittled and taken over by the factory system, and small and medium craft firms working to support and supply the factory system, as well as the fundamental difference regarding the training of

17   Theodor Geiger, *Soziale Gliederung*..., p. 103.

41

the workforce through apprenticeships. Geiger said: "As craft firms rediscover their role both within and alongside the large organisation economy and are able to consolidate their position, they are also able to regain a sense of security and dignity", and: "the crafts sector looks like strengthening in the near future, once the economic situation has calmed down, and the wave of giant industrial organisations has lessened in size. This does not mean, however, that there will be an expansion in the number of craft firms".[18]

Despite being aware that "the new middle classes should be gauged in terms not of income but of the university qualification of their work",[19] Geiger ascribed limited importance to the *freie Intelligenz,* which made up just 2% of the new middle classes, 25% of whom were proletaroids.

Schumpeter believed that the *Intelligenz* was the driving force behind modernisation processes, whereas Geiger countered that the growth in academic education and the increase in "human capital" did not appear to be underlying trends of social and cultural relevance.

Hans Speier and criticism of the concept of "proletaroid"

Following on from the studies of Lederer, Kracauer and Tobis, one of Lederer's assistants in Berlin,

---

18   Theodor Geiger, *Soziale Gliederung*..., pp. 87–88.
19   Theodor Geiger, *Soziale Gliederung*..., p. 42.

Hans Speier, wrote a very insightful essay on clerical workers, based on his personal experience in the publishing world and his trade union activity. The manuscript was given to Enke Verlag for publication by Geiger, who spoke about it very enthusiastically. But now Hitler had been in power for six months, and the negative opinion expressed by a pro-Nazi reader prevented the text from being published. It was published incomplete under the title, *The Salaried Employee in Modern Society,* during his exile in New York (Speier was one of the founders of the New School for Social Research). It would be published in Germany, revised and re-edited, only in 1977, thanks to the efforts of Jürgen Kocka. It is worth spending some time on this and other writings by Speier, as they deal directly or indirectly with the question of self-employment.[20]

Twenty years after Lederer's initial studies, the questions surrounding the "new" employee-based middle class were always the same: would the new clerical middle class move towards a proletarian mindset or remain proud of its status; would it strengthen a section of the new bourgeoisie or become part of the conservative and nationalistic movements? The history of the *Angestellten* (production and control engineers

---

20 The history of Speier's manuscript in the introduction to Hans Speier's postwar edition, *Die Angestellten vor dem Nationalsozialismus. Ein Beitrag zum Verständnis der deutschen Sozialstruktur 1918-1933* (Göttingen: Vandenhoeck § Ruprecht, 1977).

of industry and services, office staff, clerical workers in the sales sector, etc.) mirrors the whole tragedy of Weimar and the dream that a class originating from the modern era could finally form the radical-progressive bourgeoisie that had always been lacking in German history. The various strands of "white-collar" workers had given rise to a strong process of unionisation in the period after World War I. For a short time, groups of technicians and intellectuals had been attracted by councilist utopias, by the ideas of council-based self-management. Two major organisations were founded, Afa-Bund, connected to social democratic unions, and DHV, Deutschnationale Handlungsgehilfen Verband, a corporative organisation of commercial-sector clerical workers linked to Christian-social groups, and not open to female workers. The unionisation rate was, therefore, very high throughout the Weimar era, but one of the two main trade unions openly sided with the conservative and nationalist parties, including the German National Party or German People's Party. Even though collective bargaining had replaced individual bargaining, even though Rationalisation had impoverished "white-collar" more than "blue collar" workers, even though the majority of clerical workers and technicians in 1926–27 did not have higher wages than a skilled factory worker, the clerical class remained anchored to a position and to claims which, even when formulated by Afa-Bund, always sought to defend its status, emphasising its separateness from the working class.

Before he delved into the question of new technicians and clerical workers, Speier had looked at the question of self-employed workers in an essay published in "Archiv", in which he firmly rejected the dualist vision of society propounded by Marxist "orthodoxy" (capitalistic bourgeoisie and proletariat), and cast doubt on the analytical functionality of the term "middle class".[21] The figures of self-employed worker, civil servant, unemployed and employee all appeared to him difficult to fit into the schematic of Marxist *vulgate* and best illustrated the unsustainability of such a concept. He then examined these figures separately, beginning with self-employed workers, and within this group choosing the owners of commercial, agricultural or craft enterprises without employees, and with the possible presence of unpaid family workers: "they are independent because, like the unemployed, they do not have the possibility of becoming employees and are neither 'capitalists' nor 'proletarians'. If we were to rigidly apply the class theory, they should be one and the other".[22] But one precludes the other: if they are "capitalist" owners of means of production, they must deploy other people's labour to make their capital work, and if they are "proletarians", they cannot be anything else; thus these figures "lie outside the framework of class theory". To justify their existence, theory says they are "persons

---

21   Hans Speier, 'Bemerkungen zur Erfassung der sozialen
      Struktur', *ASS*, 69, 6, 705–725.
22   Hans Speier, *Bemerkungen zur...*, p. 708.

that *are not yet part* of the capitalist society", they exist *alongside the classes* as social leftovers of a previous society that was technically and economically less developed. With such an analytical procedure, Marxist "orthodoxy" (let's not forget that Speier and other authors of that time describe the official doctrine of social democracy thusly) undervalues the social role of this mass of persons, and thus also its political role, leaving them in a grey zone and applying the epitaph "petit bourgeoisie" (*Kleinbürgertum*). Since economic theory does not contemplate the co-existence of different economic systems and assigns the role of the only possible economic system to the large factory system, for the present time and even more so for the future, sociological and political theory erases, sidelines and forgets the very existence of this mass of people. Speier said that to understand how misleading this thinking was, it should be remembered that the political weight of these so-called "petit bourgeois" is greater than their economic weight in a parliamentary democracy with direct suffrage. Taking as an example German craft firms of the 1920s, small craft firms generated 18% of domestic trade sales, yet provided 29.2% of jobs in the industrial sector.

Speier went on to examine the concept of "proletaroid", noting that this concept does not belong to class theory. It is a kind of expedient by which, being unable to explain the present, an attempt is made to predict the future. "Proletaroids" are defined as those persons that appear to be in a condition whereby, in the future, they are more likely to end up among the destitute rather than the wealthy. He added that the conceptual mistake being made was that of treating "proletarians" and "proletaroids" in the same way based on their standard of living and income levels.

One of Marx's merits, Speier adds, was that of making a clear distinction between the figure of "proletarian" and that of "poor person". And he concluded: "Self-employed workers are *inside* the production process, in its broadest sense of production and movement. They cannot, however, be likened to any class since they do not have access, for now at least, to a capitalist labour market".

A class without an identity. Speier's concept of soziale Geltung

So Speier, like his mentor Lederer, tended to view self-employed workers as a mass that was destined to lose its formal independence and specific mentality, and to join the universe of subordinate employment, by assimilating its basic traits. His criticism of the idea of *Mittelstand* as a class with its own physiognomy, as a "relief valve" and "clearing house" between the two opposing classes, caused him to introduce the Weberian category of *soziale Geltung* (the translation, "social prestige", is acceptable providing one remembers that the German term indicates a set of values and lifestyles, making up the *status* that makes a given social group or stratum recognisable) and to put forward the vision of a society in which different

47

forces attempt to impose their own specific *Geltung* as a collective order. Some groups have a more marked social prestige, for instance senior military officials, who seek to prolong and defend the privileges of the military caste, whose strength lies not in the privileges juridically granted to it nor in its economic strength, but in the extent to which the sets of values recognised within the group confers an identity to its members. The clerical class represents the exact opposite, according to Speier: no matter how vital its role in the production and movement of goods, its social prestige is extremely weak, and it could be defined as *eine wert-parasitische Schicht*, a parasitic class that lives off the values of others.

Speier's essay is a treasure trove of very insightful observations regarding social stratification and flexibility tools. Some examples: "The typical means of social promotion for the white-collar worker of the past was that which led him to be independent... with the crisis, the prospect of becoming self-employed has lost all its attraction. Self-employed workers coming out of the crisis are in actual fact an atomised mass of the socially downgraded", and "Already in the period of hyperinflation, entrepreneurs sought to turn their permanent representatives into 'independent agents' who, like a normal sales representative, assume all of the risk and live on commissions".[23] At times of growth and market expansion, when the amount of commissions is likely to exceed a salary, the

---

23   Hans Speier, *Die Angestellten...*, pp. 52–53.

entrepreneur seeks to keep them as salaried workers, thus this early form of "outsourcing" that Speier is describing happens only if it entails a downgrade (*Abstieg*). Also interesting is the fact that after the rationalisation and throughout the Great Depression the percentage of unemployed technicians was higher than that for clerical workers, as if technical knowledge had become much more obsolete and surplus to requirements than the meanderings of red tape. The dream of white-collar workers working in private enterprises of attaining the same *status* as civil servants remained just that. Going against the ideas of Kracauer, who stressed the importance of higher education in the training of white-collar workers and the new bourgeoisie of the Weimar republic, Speier recalled that, in those years in Germany, 59.1% of male clerical workers and 65.8% of female possessed only secondary school qualifications.

Once the observations on self-employed workers have been put into historical perspective, what stands out about Speier's analysis is the great wisdom shown regarding the concept of social prestige, which we might transfer to modern-day thinking through the concept of *identity*, replacing the idea of prestige with that of "recognisability and visibility". Having a similar role in the production process, the same level of education, a similar level of income and the same standard of living are not in themselves enough to make two persons into two members of the same class or the same social stratum. They are not proletariats, and they are not middle class, however you might wish it — this appears to be the teaching from these sociologists who sought to dismantle the sterile schematics of Marxist vulgate spouted repeatedly by social democratic propaganda. The question of identity is one of mental habits, which relate only partly to "objective, quantifiable and statistically measurable conditions". The 19th century self-employed workers analysed by Lederer in the 1913 essay still appeared to have their social recognition while those of the Great Depression analysed by Speier had lost it: they were unemployed workers trying to make ends meet by performing self-employed activities.

Middle classes, self-employed workers and national socialism (Nazism). A note

The social democrats had mistaken the strong drive of white-collar workers to organise themselves in trade unions for an "inclination to proletarisation", but the search for class identity is something that transcends the defending of common interests in relations with the employer and the state. As the average wage of white-collar workers fell, as unemployment became more common and lasted longer, it was believed that solidarity with factory workers and unemployed former factory workers was destined to grow. However, Speier believed that, more than income, these "petits bourgeois" sought social prestige, an identity to measure up to other "strong" identities, that of unionised blue-collar workers, unemployment

50

benefit recipients, soldiers, civil servants, university professors and intellectuals. Not having found this, not having managed to develop with their own kind a *Stilverwandschaft*, having lost every hope of social promotion, frustrated, disgruntled, impotent, organised in unions but politically invisible, they threw themselves into the arms of the Nazis. "A study of electoral results in the Weimar republic confirms that white-collar workers were very receptive to the calls of Nazi propaganda. The NSDAP received very few votes from blue-collar workers and, more than anybody else, from self-employed workers, particularly in the cities. Self-employed workers in industry and commerce were particularly enthusiastic. No less enthusiastic, however, were public sector white-collar workers and civil servants."[24] The last sentence was probably added after the war when Speier's text was revised.

Theodor Geiger had already examined the relationship between self-employed workers and voting for the Nazis in a well-known article published in "Die Arbeit" after the general elections of 1930 (when the Nazis suddenly won more than a hundred seats in the Reichstag). The article is entitled *Panik im Mittelstand*, panic among the middle classes, and has partly been translated into Italian in the anthology edited by Mariuccia Salvati.[25] The social group

---

24   Hans Speier, *Die Angestellten...*, pp. 119–120.
25   Theodor Geiger, 'Panik im Mittelstand', *Die Arbeit*, 10 (1930), 638–654; Mariuccia Salvati, *Da Berlino a New York*, pp. 143 et seq.

on which focus continued to be placed was that of white-collar workers. The interpretation offered by Geiger is that the push to vote for the Nazis came from *Angst vor Mindereinschätzung*, the fear of being held in less regard, the fear of a loss of social prestige on the part of all categories: civil servants, white-collar workers as children of self-employed workers, white-collar workers as children of blue-collar workers, self-employed workers downgraded by the crisis, and soldiers. Although rich in sagacious observations, Geiger's article took it for granted that the defenders of democracy were the working classes and that the increase in numbers voting for the Nazis was attributable to the "old" and the "new" middle classes. But he concluded very optimistically: "Is there the danger of a counter-revolution? Everything appears to say no. Notwithstanding the way the wind is blowing, a revolution of the middle classes does not start like this. To have a revolution, what is needed is not only everyone wanting to work together, but also some constructive ideas. The Third Reich is not an idea, it is a hollow phrase." And then the theory of opposing extremisms: "The frightening pressure exerted on workers by the economic crisis has caused anger and outbursts (*Rabiatismus*): workers towards communists, ideologically disoriented white-collar workers towards Nazis. An unemployed factory worker wants Moscow, an unemployed clerical worker the Third Reich."[26]

---

26   Theodor Geiger, *Panik im Mittelstand*, pp. 653–654.

Three years later Geiger would be forced to revise his optimistic forecasts, yet he would not alter his interpretation. Following the victory of Nazism, the political ideas of exiles would form the basic principles of the ideology of German leaders after World War II. In this ideology, the theorem of the middle classes, the main supporters of national socialism, would be an important chapter in the new social democratic *vulgate*. As a component of both the "old" and "new" middle classes, self-employment would have to drag this stigma behind them and would continue to be considered, in the repeated stupidity of the left, as a breeding ground for reactionary rebellion.[27]

We should not end this review without mentioning a text that was very important in sanctioning the hypothesis that the German white-collar class had been, together with "new" middle classes, the social base of Nazism. This text is the monumental research conducted by Jürgen Kocka on American white-collar workers.[28] Kocka, one of the founders of the new social history (*neue Sozialgeschichte*), re-published Lederer's texts in the late 1970s and edited the first German edition of Speier's text forty-four years after it was written. Kocka's research thus comes from

---

27 Theodor Geiger, *Die soziale Schichtung...*, pp. 109 et seq. One of the important questions examined by Weimarian sociology was that of social mobility; see Svend Riemer, 'Sozialer Aufstieg und Klassenschichtung', *ASS*, 67, 5, 531–560.

28 See note 12.

the same historical-political tradition and in a way seeks to provide further proof of Speier, Lederer and Geiger's opinions regarding the relationship between the middle classes and national socialism. The reason for the alliance between white-collar workers, the "new middle class" and NSDAP lay, as we have seen, in the fact that white-collar workers had not been able to develop a class identity; they had been crushed by the strength of other identities, other "state" cultures, other caste ideologies, and had thus been forced to steal the values, lifestyles and mindsets of classes that did not share their professional or social role. The legacy of pre-capitalist mentalities and the failure to modernise these mentalities was believed to have been behind the conversion of the "new middle classes" to Nazism, in particular white-collar workers in Taylorist companies. Kocka's research into American white-collar workers sought to demonstrate that in the United States the modernisation of the capitalist organisation and of class cultures was progressing at an equal pace. American white-collar workers managed to develop their own class identity, social values, lifestyles, and customs in keeping with their social stratum and of no other, and thus, having a moral certitude about their social recognition, identified more readily with the form of government and production model that had allowed them to make this social affirmation. Thanks to Kocka's authority, as a leading light in the Bielefeld school of historians, and the philological rigour of his research (only a small part of the documentation consulted is given in the bibliography of the Italian edition), Lederer and Speier's ideas were legitimised in full. Their interpretations regarding the social determinants behind Hitler's coming to power were thus reinforced, and the categories of "middle class" and "self-employed worker" lost their sociological connotations. They became ideal-typical figures symbolising the attitudes and behaviour of subversive rebellion, and undergoing the same change of meaning as that undergone early in the century by the "proletariat" category, which went from being the name of a social class to the definition of a political stance. Kocka himself reminded us that most concepts of the historical and social sciences derive from a context in which practical and ideological factors are closely entwined with theoretical and scientific factors.

From the 1930s to the 1970s, the rise and fall of the Fordist model

Studies on self-employment, abandoned when the Nazis came to power, resumed in the late 1970s. Such studies had begun in the first decade of the century when the Taylorist-Fordist paradigm had first appeared and sociologists had begun to document the demise of self-employment and the transformation of society into a salaried society. They had disappeared when the Taylorist-Fordist system was no longer met with opposition in the West and had been introduced and glorified in the USSR by Stalinist Stakhanovites. Salaried employment appeared to be the only possible form of citizenship in industrial nations, while self-employment was considered as a "reserve army" pending enrolment in the salaried work system. What is more, self-employment was suspected of being a breeding ground for all "conservative revolutions", the residue of a pre-capitalist and pre-democratic past, part of the *ancien régime*.

Once they had emigrated to the United States, the Weimarian sociologists changed their vantage point. Emil Lederer, Hans Speier and many others found it necessary to examine more deeply the question of mass culture in order to gain a better understanding of the crisis of democracy. A study of the internal composition of classes did not appear to answer the question of how Nazism and Fascism had taken hold in Europe.[29] Theodor Geiger chose to go and

---

29 Mariuccia Salvati, *Da Berlino a New York*, gives a rich bibliography on the subject of emigration and the progressive integration between researchers from Germany or Austria and American researchers. As this subject is not central to this work, I have not updated this bibliography, which stops at 1988–89. A relevant aspect of the "new" middle classes is that regarding the role of professions and "technicians" in general, a topic that Alfredo Salsano in Italy has tackled on several occasions, in his book *Ingegneri e politici* (Turin: Einaudi, 1987), and introductory essays to the Italian edition of J. Burnham, *La rivoluzione manageriale* (Turin: Bollati Boringhieri, 1992), and the writings of J. Schumpeter, *L'imprenditore e la storia dell'impresa, Scritti 1927-1949* (Turin: Bollati Boringhieri, 19939. The tenth volume of *Storia d'Italia* (Turin: Einaudi, 1996), ed.

live in Denmark, where he studied bureaucracy and intellectuals, but did not totally turn his back on sociography. In the United Kingdom, Karl Mannheim focused more on the question of complexity and how to govern it in democratic terms.

Things changed after the war. The mass parties, the parties of social democrats, communists, Catholics and liberals that emerged in European countries previously governed by Fascism and Nazism, organised themselves as mixed-class parties. Workers' trade unions multiplied their cultural and ideological elements, becoming communist, socialist, social democratic, Catholic. The middle classes formed the backbone of Western European society, the part of the electorate fought over by all parties, the basis of democracy and political stability. Communist parties, too, sought to win them over, seeking to reconcile their interests with those of the working class. The image of a middle class posing a danger to democratic stability is one that fades and disappears in the mind, while self-employment increasingly looks like a "leftover" of a bygone era and is identified with everything that is not modernisation.

Studies on self-employment came back into fashion when the capitalist organisation changed, with the

---

by M. Malatesta, is wholly dedicated to *I professionisti*; see also *Libere professioni e fascismo*, ed. by Gabriele Turi (Milan: Angeli, 1994), and Francesca Tarchi, 'I professionisti italiani tra tradizione e modernità›, *Passato e Presente*, 40 (1997), 133–142.

affirmation of a new production model, which we have provisionally called *Post-Fordist*. This new form of production and distribution appears to need a society of independent, unsalaried workers. The result is a new generation of self-employment.

The interpretations we have already made about Weimarian sociology and sociography have shown that first, second and third generation are definitions that have little do with biology; they are sociological characterisations that indicate change within a social and productive area — the "old" and "new" *Mittelstand*, the "old" and "new" crafts: the "old" 19th century self-employment anchored to the ownership of means of production, possession of land, a commercial space, and a means of transport; and the "new" self-employment of the late 1920s made up of workers that have been downgraded or made unemployed. Self-employment thus underwent radical changes from the 1930s onwards, varying from country to country. As a reconstruction of this evolution would take us away from the focus of this essay, I will focus on the period in which the first earth tremors were felt, loosening the all-powerful productive paradigm in place for three quarters of a century. I will focus on the 1970s, the period when the crisis of the Taylorist-Fordist model was perceived. The two cases I will refer to, and which I have direct experience of, present too many similarities to claim that it was pure coincidence.

From protests to the art of getting by: the post-1968 generation in Italy

The first is the Italian case. In the final days of the student protest movement, in the second half of the 1970s, there was a great crisis in the credibility of revolutionary ideologies inspired by the history of communism, and the first signs of a radical restructuring process were appearing that would go on to affect the large factories. The 1968 generation began to look with interest at the creation of "alternative" forms of existence. The enthusiasm and hopes of 1968 had faded, the idea of "politics" as the total participation of the individual had lost its attractiveness. Moreover, the strong drive towards self-organisation and performance of self-managed cultural activities had formed a slender backdrop that might serve as a launchpad for building life "alternatives" in accordance with the more traditional formula of self-employment. The energies expended in taking an active part in politics, the custom of cultivating utopian thoughts, a certain experience in bringing life to clubs/associations, newspapers and social centres gave many people of that generation a certain confidence in their own abilities, which was crucial for those intending to take up the adventure of self-employment. The term "alternative" that was used for many of these initiatives was often a disguise to conceal the "false conscience" of those going from revolutionary utopias to a "petit bourgeois" existence. It cannot be denied, however, that this transition, of little significance in quantitative terms but quite significant culturally and in terms of a change in mindset, as it was happening to a generation that had great public visibility, has been seen, from an ideological viewpoint, as a way of satisfying that desire for freedom and independence that had been behind the support given by many to the protest movements. This trend was driven not only by those choosing to go into more traditional forms of self-employment, such as retailing and catering — which in some cases led to the establishment of successful companies — but also by those who had a new vision of professional ethics, based on beliefs acquired through a complex process of theoretical and practical experience. There was, for example, criticism of healthcare and the role played by healthcare staff, more general "criticism of science" and "criticism of technologies", and "criticism of traditional disciplines". Many people were quietly confident they could go into productive activities or services using "alternative" techniques and knowledge and offer to the market "innovative" goods and services.[30]

---

30 I believe the work of the editorial staff of the journal, "Sapere", directed by Giulio Maccacaro, can be included in these "tendencies of the age". While it is true that this experience, of which I was a part, was basically aimed at researchers, academics and social workers, all working in public sector employment, i.e., in the area of guaranteed work, it is also true that it was the most technical-specialist part of the change in mentality, the part that produced a more "mature" sort of innovation. Alongside this was the part that involved "grassroots activists", less innovative in terms of

The liberation from salaried work, overcoming a mindset that appeared to be the only possibility in modern capitalist society, and a mentality that viewed subordinate labour as the natural form of work, freeing oneself from a cultural legacy that had been constructed in equal measure by Western capitalism and Soviet socialism: these could all be handled more easily by a generation that carried a very strong utopian vision and an equally ambitious social vision. The belief that there were sufficient human resources to tackle the challenge of non-salaried employment was accompanied by the paranoid refusal of many to join organisations in which work was founded on respect for procedures and hierarchies. There was thus a complex and contradictory set of motivations: those that had become complacent, those that had thrown in the towel ("Let's get rich!"), those who, not having succeeded in eliminating the bosses, wanted at least in their personal life not to have one, those convinced they had, with their "alternative" techniques, a competitive edge, those convinced that activism had condemned them to life as an outsider, those clinging to a return to normality to escape the temptation — quite common back then — of launching themselves into suicidal "armed struggle", and those, perhaps the

---

theory and more pragmatic in the art of getting by, situated on a social level in the area of precarious and non-guaranteed employment. So, within this transformation of mentalities, we do indeed find a social stratification and a difference in status, but also a strong process of osmosis in terms of experiences.

61

majority, who believed they had developed, thanks to their "out-of-the-ordinary" political and organisational experiences, some special people-handling skills.[31]

The 1968 generation (here we use the term "generation" bearing in mind Mannheim's thoughts about the "generation problem") generally had little faith in their technical and professional resources, thinking perhaps they had sacrificed their studies for other things, but had great faith in their *relational* capabilities. It was, therefore, a workforce that was particularly suited to the services and media society. For a number of complex reasons, many of the positive and negative traits that form the necessary requirements for the creation of self-employment

---

31   The considerations contained in this paragraph are based on personal experience, having participated for more than a decade in the experiences of the 1968 generation and personally in self-managed, non-profit, "alternative" initiatives in the cultural sphere. In actual fact, the term "1968 generation" may be misleading as far as the Italian situation is concerned. In other countries, particularly in the United States and France, student protests did not last as long and did not trigger a process of permanent conflict in factories and the services sector, as they did in Italy. Thus the flow of people entering and exiting protest and political struggle movements or forming political groups in and out of parliament and in and out of trade unions lasted for more than a decade in Italy and involved a considerable number of people. There was not, despite assertions to the contrary, a season of "reflux" and one of "activism", there was a sort of self-regeneration that fuelled outgoing flows (and thus people choosing self-employment) for about a decade.

were thus concentrated in this social stratum. Initiatives regarding self-employment related only partly to individual firms and partnerships: many initiatives took the form of cooperatives, allowing the "false conscience" of their members to think of their experience as a sort of reborn socialism, conferring on the life of the individual a sort of continuity with the ideals of the past, and not an embarrassing sense of breaking from the past. With the cooperative form, resources could be organised better, and there was a more mature perception of the market compared with the individual enterprise form.

Blue-collar workers, too, had a say in creating independent work, albeit less visibly.

Such cases represent the clearest form of breakaway from the status of salaried worker, hierarchical subordination, and procedures and forms of regulation. Blue-collar workers, in particular Fordist factory workers, do not appear to possess the requirements needed to enter the sphere of self-employment, particularly knowledge resources. It is a cliché that the area of crafts and minor repairs is the only sector of self-employment in which their resources are adequate. In actual fact, the generation of skilled workers formed during the course of trade union conflicts in the early 1970s had developed the same relational skills as student activists, and had greater manual skills. Among blue-collar workers, the rejection of salaried employment was more a rebellion against factory rules than an aspiration for a higher standard of living or quality of life. In many cases, it was more a resignation than a dismissal, owing to the defeat of more radical conflict practices and to marginalisation from factory rules and even workmates. It is not possible to gauge the extent to which laid-off workers moved to the area of self-employment as no systematic studies have been conducted in this respect. The cases we have come across appear to indicate that, by creating a state of "occupational limbo", the condition of being made redundant blocked rather than encouraged a spirit of initiative, facilitating not only irregular employment but also a move towards another salaried job or towards early retirement rather than self-employment. Nevertheless, there were more than a few blue-collar workers active in trade unions in the factory, in the front line of industrial conflict and possessing radical ideologies, that would go on to become micro-entrepreneurs, adding to the panorama of a generation which, characterised by "proletarisation" and radicalisation of the dichotomous vision of society (capital-class), ended up being one of the driving forces for workers' exit from salaried employment and the Taylorist-Fordist model.

Escaping the regulated working day in the ideologies of the "1977 movement"

Perception of this change of paradigm was a cultural process that developed from the thoughts of some intellectuals, and should in any case be kept separate from the spontaneous actions of individuals. It should come as no surprise that the small group of intellectuals that anticipated the change in paradigm came from the experience of so-called "Italian workerism", i.e., groups that reflected and acted on political issues and that brought back to life in Italy the "sociology of the classes", seeking to create a change in the status of the intellectual.[32] Thanks to direct "grassroots" experience, they were able to grasp better than others the nature and internal dynamics of late-Fordism, reflecting on international experiences, primarily in Germany and the United States. The "sociology of the classes" returned to the fore with the "blue-collar worker survey", the return to empirical research or, as those in and around the "Quaderni Rossi", would say,

---

32 The story has never been written of the group of intellectuals from the journal "Quaderni Rossi" and then "Classe Operaia", who came to participate directly in the 1968 student protests and worker struggles, from the creation of local committees to the "hot autumn" of 1969, then taking part in the grassroots movements of the 1970s and the experience of "criticism of the disciplines" up to the 1977 movement and the final struggles in Fiat (1980). Having participated in all these experiences in the twenty-year period from 1960 to 1980, I refer the reader to the autobiographical notes contained in *Memorie di un operaista*, published in the monthly supplements of "Il Manifesto", dedicated to the 1968 movement twenty years later (1988). As regards the subsequent period, in particular the story of my ties with Germany and "alternative" German movements of the 1980s, I refer to the introduction to the second edition of my essay, *Nazismo e classe operaia. 1933-1993* (Rome: manifestolibri, 1997), pp. 9–62.

to "joint research". The hovering cloud of Stalinism and Togliattism was thus dispersed with a "split" to the left. Luckily, some interlocutors were found in that part of the industrial world (Italsider, ENI, Olivetti), which, towards the late 1950s, had begun to modernise human resource management techniques and managerial practices.

Some of that group of intellectuals had been through the rise and decline of the protest movements, had been present or taken part directly in the so-called "reflux" phase, and had noted the spontaneous choice of many people to become "autonomous" in the labour market. But to be certain of a change in mentality, and to mark the beginning of a new era, confirmation was needed that only a social movement could give.

It may have been fleeting, but the so-called "1977 movement" yielded such a confirmation, highlighting the fact that young people ten years younger than the 1968 generation were even more driven to escape from regulated employment, permanent employment and a regulated working day. The utopia of independence and the liberation from control (the symbolism of "travel", glorification of the "vagabond" and infatuation with America) appeared to be oriented, primarily, against forms of political or social organisation founded on discipline, official regulations and conformism. Unlike the ideologies of the 1968 generation that wanted to see "real communism" come to fruition, for the youngsters of 1977 communism was a negative model, the social form of factory discipline. Historical institutions of the worker movement (trade unions, PCI) were heavily criticised as being representatives of the social order founded on dependent and regulated employment. The Berlin wall started coming down at that time too, taking with it the social prestige of salaried employment. The reaction of the PCI was furious and unwise: it considered those youngsters as *asozial*, the same way they considered potential terrorists, and failed to appreciate that they simply represented the other face of industrial districts, the workforce of the poor tertiary sector and service companies, the reserve army of flexibility and precarious employment.[33]

Italian industrial districts and the way they are represented in economic sociology

In that period, the second half of the 1970s, in the zones of the so-called "third Italy" (Veneto, Emilia-Romagna, Tuscany, Marche), district systems where flexible production was being developed gave rise to "Italian-style Post-Fordism". This system was to be

---

33   The journal, "Primo Maggio", was undoubtedly one of the centres of thought that considered these phenomena, offering ideas and working hypotheses; see the contributions collected in the volume, *La tribù delle talpe* (Milan: Feltrinelli, 1978). From September 1975 to the end of 1977, Franco Berardi's ("Bifo") journal, "A/ Traverso", and, in the period 1976–77, the journal, "Lotta continua", directed by Enrico Deaglio devoted numerous articles to the topic of alternative economies and to forms of unsalaried work.

one of the main sources of self-employment creation, especially in the form of craft firms.[34] The formation of industrial districts and the relevance ascribed to them by business economists and industrial sociologists represent a historical event, the scope of which certainly cannot be compared to the changes in mentality brought about by the protest movements, either quantitatively or qualitatively, but it is nevertheless true that they helped, paradoxically, to draw a veil over rather

---

34 General conclusions have not been reached about the researches conducted by economists and sociologists on industrial districts. Here we might recall only the main centres of research, which have the merit of outlining the traits of the district "model": the university of Florence, coordinated by Giacomo Becattini, offering an annual review of the relative situation in the "Incontri pratesi"; the University of Modena, coordinated by Sebastiano Brusco; the Industrial Policy Laboratory of the Bologna-based company Nomisma, coordinated by Patrizio Bianchi; the Faculty of Economics of the University of Venice, coordinated by Enzo Rullani; the Department of Local Economics and Science of the University of Venice, coordinated by Francesco Indovina, and more recently the Faculty of Economics of the University of Naples, coordinated by Luca Meldolesi. Of the more recent and important contributions to the district question, see B. Anastasia, G. Coro, *Evoluzione di un'economia regionale. Il Nord Est dopo il successo* (Pordenone: Ediciclo editore, 1996), and Paolo Perulli's address, *Capitalismi italiani e Postfordismo*, presented in April 1996 at the triennial conference of the Italian Association of Sociology, Economics, Employment and Organisation (typewritten, pp. 19).

than highlight self-employment. Clearly, here we are talking chiefly about how this system was represented, going back to the theories of the English economist Alfred Marshall, who at the beginning of the century had spoken about local systems of small-medium enterprises as an alternative to the development of systems having a large industrial concentration. How is it possible for an economic form that has played a key role in establishing the Post-Fordist model (networks of enterprises, outsourcing, subcontracting, flexibility, osmosis of innovative processes, formation of the micro-enterprise, promotion of "new" or "modern" crafts under the terms that Schumpeter had already identified in the 1920s) to be represented and theorised in such a way as to conceal the phenomenon of self-employment? In a way, the answer is quite simple: there is a big difference between considering the same economic entity, a micro-enterprise for example, as work or as an enterprise. It entails entering semantic fields that are not only profoundly different but also culturally antithetical. Representing industrial districts as the most efficient and dynamic capitalist production model capable of guaranteeing social cohesion meant putting the emphasis on entrepreneurial spirit, on the optimism of profit, on wealth generated, on wellbeing acquired, and not on the energy spent or consumption of the workforce. Representing the enterprise meant giving coverage to success, representing work meant highlighting the sweat and tears. The effort and inventiveness used to find out the reasons behind the success of small enterprises working in industrial

69

districts appeared to seek to erase the effort with which reasons were sought for the unhappiness of workers on the assembly line.[35] It is not, however, possible to talk only about different representations of reality. Social behaviour was actually different. The Fiat factory worker, confined to a "wage" that, despite years of struggles, grew very slowly, was a social type not dissimilar to the worker in the clothing factory who sets up his own business, driven by the same firm he

---

35 Marino Regini made a significant contribution to the way in which economic sociologists have interpreted SME systems; see 'È davvero in crisi la sociologia economica?', *Sociologia del lavoro,* 61 (September 1996), pp. 116–120. Regini states: "Italian researchers have been at the cutting edge in developing this important research topic [on industrial districts and the hidden economy — *author's note*] and in suggesting the role to be played by institutions and social networks, helped by the fact that Italy is particularly abundant in such phenomena, which cannot be explained in traditional ways. How to explain the spread of small enterprises in the richest parts of the country, where civil society is more organised and endowed with resources, rather than in poorer, socially disintegrated areas? And how to explain the fact that most of these small enterprises do not have the expected characteristics of marginality, low labour costs and labour-intensive organisation, but often compete in terms of quality, design and technological innovation, employ highly qualified, well paid and union card-carrying personnel? The interpretations of these Italian traits have rightly centred on the institutional setting, calling into question the roles of the family, sub-cultural and community networks, associations and local institutions." (ibid., p. 120).

was employed by, and who saw a growth in his "sales revenue" in a few years. In the late 1970s, when this transformation took place, the Fordist model appeared more than anything to be a pile of conflicts and class hatred, while the Post-Fordist district model appeared to be a peaceful micro-universe. The presence of the "red threat" in the major industrial centres of the country (Turin, Genoa, Milan, Marghera) was decisive in creating a black cloud over the Fordist model.

The changes to the status of work thus went unnoticed: the Fiat worker worked eight hours a day, with paid overtime, while the family of the craftsman with the numerical control machine in the garage worked 24 hours a day. "Working hours of twelve hours a day, weekends and bank holidays included, appear to be routine", a Nomisma research on industrial districts noted, almost incidentally, in the late 1980s. Sociologists and economists came from all over the world to observe, analyse and extol the miracle of Italian industrial districts. The international renown of some of our sociologists and economists indeed was basically due to the work done marketing the district model. It was indeed a "miracle": spirit of initiative, speed in interiorising new technologies, daring leaps into overseas markets, imaginative product innovation and, even more significantly, the organisation of new networked systems, and the clever use of institutions and university research. We really are able to say, without being rhetorical, that this was a capitalist "Renaissance". A class of new entrepreneurs, with a different mindset, rooted in the manufacturing process, was born and multiplied, enhancing the role of smaller towns, which encouraged social cohesion, new "centres" of this system, as opposed to the declining metropolises, producers of social disintegration, reduced to being "peripheral".

Looking from our current standpoint, this contrast probably seems to be naive, over-simplistic, and the "miracle" of the industrial districts, compared with general conditions, appears to be a little less miraculous, especially if one considers that the success of small and medium enterprises in Italian industrial districts was determined by a) the presence of foreign buyers, especially German, who provided a steady outlet market, b) an Italian monetary policy that, through the payment of high interest rates on government securities, flooded the domestic market with spendable cash, such as to drive internal consumption and investment income.

The way the success of industrial districts was represented probably now appears to be unilateral, and the managerial approach insufficient, but even the most critical voices of the "district model", such as American Bennett Harrison in his book, *Lean and Mean,* (Harrison was one of the very few to raise the problem of "work", albeit salaried, in industrial districts), focused on the analysis of processes of financial re-concentration, with the consequent reassessment of the large enterprise model as an entity capable of generating profit and innovation. Thus we find ourselves, on the one hand, still disputing what is best between "large" and "small" and, on the other, balancing the sense of excessive euphoria pervading the 1980s decade with a sense of pessimism resulting from the crisis of the 1990s. The representation of small and medium enterprise systems highlights not their merits but their limitations.[36] In my opinion, the picture given of industrial districts and "Italian-style Post-Fordism" has always been partial, to the extent that we have never been made to "see" the changes to the social status of work, but merely observed the engineering of widespread profit. It has also erased from the physiognomy of the micro-entrepreneur the traits of the worker, has been unable to make out the very thin line between success and poverty, and not wanted to "see" the latency of the hardships involved. In short, it has been unable to grasp the ambiguity of self-employment. In the extensive literature on industrial districts, the very

---

36   *"What's wrong with the 'small firms' story?"*, Ben Harrison asks. "But economists and sociologists now almost universally (if reluctantly) agree that since the 1970s the distribution of income has been changing its shape again, becoming an hourglass with an expanding upper end of well-paid professionals (including Reich's 'symbolic analysts') a growing mass of low-paid workers at the bottom, and a shrinking middle class of increasingly downwardly mobile former factory workers and middle managers made redundant by the philosophy of lean production." (chap. I of *Lean and Mean*, Basic Books, New York 1993, typewritten). As can be seen from this quote, even the critics of the small and medium enterprise myth are unable to abandon the way of thinking about salaried work, reasoning within the confines of Labour tradition, typical of both the "old" and "new" left.

term "self-employment" appears extremely rarely. But this "blindness" is typical of those who went from the optimism of the 1980s to the pessimism of the 1990s. Both those who continue, unfazed, to believe in the "magnificent progression" of SME systems and in their ability to foster social cohesion, and those who note the comeback of the large enterprise and highlight the ever greater gap between rich and poor, between the rich and the impoverished middle classes, continue to wear the "social-psychic habitus of the present" as described by Lederer at the beginning of the century. Both observe the transformation of work with the mentality of a bygone age. When, in the Italian regions where industrial districts originated, the North-east in particular, the national state first began to be delegitimised, when in the sprawling cities of the North new political organisations began to appear, such as Berlusconi's party, these same observers, reasoning with the mentality of a bygone age, looked back to the German researchers of the 1930s and their take on the conservative and rebellious nature of the "new" middle classes. They forgot all about the "sociographic" factors on which their conclusions were based, thus adding misunderstanding to misunderstanding, in a muddled verbiage, invoking the concepts of "just in time", globalisation, possessive individualism, and so on.[37]

---

37 The term "just in time" is too often used as a category of the capitalist spirit; it is actually a technical term used in industrial logistics, the management of business resources founded on keeping stock levels down. As it has evolved, it

Reflections on the neue Selbständige *in German "alternative economics" movements*

There are some curious coincidences between the German and Italian situations. The drive towards forms of self-employment came in particular from the currents of radical ecologism, mass struggles against nuclear energy and in favour of the use of "alternative", non-industrially produced power sources. Many people tend to prefer free initiative in retail trading and crafts to salaried employment in the public administration and private sector; and many prefer to live in "farming communities" and to try out organic farming rather than live life in large

---

has become a model for the management and coordination of physical flows, from procurement to the distribution of products, used to govern the growing complexity of outsourcing processes with constant flexibility. Logistics, backed by computerised and online tools, belongs to the sphere of material production; it is not a virtual material handling process but a universe in which the hardware is more important than the software. It requires high fixed capital investments and, in the segment that is most difficult to govern, freight transport; it is one of the most labour-intensive sectors, with very high exploitation rates. The network enterprise or globalisation phenomenon would be impossible without logistics and transport, i.e., without the physical links between network nodes. As self-employment is particularly common in the transport and goods handling sector, my experience, spanning ten years as a researcher and consultant in this sector, has helped me to write down some thoughts on self-employment.

urban metropolises. These ideologies and practices are not new in German history. Returning to the land or to craft trades is a phenomenon that had already emerged in the first decade of the century and became important in the Weimar republic, where everything seemed to be happening, for better or worse, under laboratory conditions. In the late 1970s, the choice of unsalaried, unregulated work outside the city was also an ideologically motivated choice, a "protest" against the runaway train of history and development. A term was coined to indicate "someone getting off the train": *Aussteiger*. The contribution of female blue-collar workers in the Italian experience should not be underestimated, and women also played a very important role in the German experience. Women's search for independence in the workplace often leads to forms of self-employment in individual firms or cooperatives. In the spheres of culture, educational services and in general personal services, the presence of women is also the result of ideological motivations. As in the Italian case, relative behaviour is sometimes ambivalent, with some "choosing" an alternative path and others "forced" to choose a path when labour market conditions are such as to leave little hope of obtaining salaried employment. As political parties became the arbiters of employment in the public administration, those implicated in one way or another in protest movements against the "system" auto-excluded themselves from a section of salaried work. In such cases, self-employment becomes a necessity. We should not forget that in the period under review

Germany's production system underwent a radical restructuring, with massive de-industrialisation phenomena in traditional sectors: heavy engineering and the chemical, iron and steel industries. Thus the prospects of finding a factory job were dwindling.

Some sociologists of Oldenburg, from their peripheral location in an area gripped by a job crisis, were the first to document this "rebirth" of self-employment driven by anti-modernist ideologies, and the first to note that while in the 1920s self-employment was strongly influenced by the "conservative revolution", in the 1970s there was the attraction of radical democracy movements (pacifism, anti-nuclear, feminism, civil rights) and libertarian and anarchic movements, and an equally strong hostility shown against the communist model. So in Germany, too, the Berlin wall started crumbling as the 1980s approached. A significant document was published in 1980 by one of the leading exponents of the Oldenburg group, Gerd Vonderach, entitled *Die 'neuen Selbständigen'. 10 Thesen zur Soziologie eines unvermuteten Phänomens* ("The 'new self-employed workers'. 10 posits for the sociology of an unannounced phenomenon").

After having examined the theoretical aspects of the concept of class and history of French utopian socialists, Vonderach came across the phenomenon of self-employment and *aussteigen* (the ideas are preceded by six "case studies" of persons in his circle of acquaintances that chose various forms of self-employment) and placed it in the framework of his criticism of the cyber/Internet society, of modernity,

77

of limitless development, theorisation of a "post-industrial" and services society, identification of a "fourth sector", that of the informal or black economy, along the lines suggested by American authors such as Bell, Gershuny, Illich, Henry and Gutman. The main recruiting ground, Vonderach believed, was that of university students, who abandoned their studies due to an explicit refusal to follow "standard professional careers". The phenomenon of "new self-employed workers" is not at odds with the industrial society, yet it indicates some alternatives to the mode of development (posit 1). The "new self-employed workers" can make up the backbone of a parallel system in which decentralised production and new forms of subsistence can create a space freed of state red tape and the rules of large industrial organisations (posit 2). The majority of "new self-employed" are not self-employed because they have inherited means of production or because it matches their training and educational path; they work on their own or in cooperative form with little or no formalisation and with short-term prospects (posit 3). The "new self-employed" do not separate private and working life; the activity they perform is partly serious, tried and tested, and partly playful and experimental (posit 4). In particular, "the new self-employed", in their private and working lives, reject the normal rationality of the workplace" (p. 161). The "new self-employed" react differently to the challenge of competitiveness, changing consumption standards and re-organising the division of labour, and they take very seriously the goals they set themselves, always seeking to change lifestyles and ways of working (posit 5). The new type of self-employment is one involving young people, in response to the lack of job opportunities and the false promises of a professional career, a reaction to the employment crisis and to the loss of the meaning of work (posit 6). It is already helping to reduce the available supply of labour and is suitable for sectors requiring a high density of labour and great flexibility, thus it should be supported with ad hoc incentive measures (posit 7). The "new self-employed" break the professional barriers and paths traced out by the public school and university education system, thus they can make a contribution to rethinking the public higher education system (posit 8). The "new self-employed" cannot be broken down by class: they are the counter-subject of the "class of experts" produced by technology, bureaucracy and scientism; they cannot be contained within the system of class interests of the old self-employed workers, as they believe they are bringing a new set of values (posit 9). They are setting a "demodernisation" trend, and are helping to build a local culture, one of self-management (posit 10).

Each posit is followed by a long explanation, thus the document is quite long for a set of "posits", and the attached bibliography shows how much the topic of the "alternative" economy had grown in popularity in the press and literature of the time. The publisher, Fischer, produced a collection entitled "alternativ", and journals that were uncompromisingly Marxist such as "Mehrwert" and journals such as "Technologie und

Politik" often examined these alternative occupations. A bibliography on the culture of "alternative economies" published in 1989 filled 700 pages of titles!

Vonderach stressed the importance of a different use of human capital, and this is the most interesting aspect of his analysis. When Geiger cited the cases of many young people that had studied at university and chosen the path of self-employment and retail trade, since the labour market situation was very much unfavourable in relation to their expectations, he demonstrated a profound disdain for the lives of these frustrated youngsters, *déracinés* of the 1920s, failed physicians, failed lawyers, failed teachers, resentful and dissatisfied. Vonderach interpreted the phenomenon as a discovery of the deception of science and the loss of credibility of higher education courses, and support of "critical sciences", alternative disciplines, a readiness to "self-study", and a search for individual and original training paths. The feeling that university for the masses is ineffective and a university degree useless, has led not only to forms of employment other than subordinate work but also to the creation of different products of work. Vonderach believed that the crisis in credibility of the path going from university studies to professional specialisation and a permanent job and career in a company, the crisis in credibility of the paradigms of sciences and different disciplines, and confidence in the ability to "teach oneself" were the main reasons behind the formation of the new class of self-employed workers, rather than any particular love for nature, the countryside or manual labour.

But Dieter Bögenhold, one of the leading experts on self-employment in Germany, he also hailing from the Oldenburg group, wrote in a publication[38] about the "alternative" of the *neue Selbständige* with sarcastic disdain, calling them ideological guises of improvised choices bereft of any real innovation. Fifteen years have passed since the writing of the two texts, during the course of which the world has changed, the views of experts have changed, the Berlin wall has fallen, and the "alternative economy" is a rare sight. Yet anyone that had the opportunity to participate in the day-to-day life of these "new self-employed" in Germany in the early 1980s can but share Vonderach's diagnosis made at the time. With the focus very much on ethics, a strong intellectual curiosity and readiness to experiment, these workers had created a veritable collective mindset, a characteristic lifestyle. It was a mindset that, while not comparable with the protestant ethic spoken about by Weber, definitely had a similar effect in creating entrepreneurial energies and shaping a different kind of "work ethic", thus it cannot be trivialised or ridiculed. If, instead of looking at the phenomenon from the viewpoint of someone expecting a palingenesis and, disappointed when this does not occur, iconoclastically destroys its past, we viewed the creation of "alternatives" simply as a group of people who, rightly or wrongly, had realised

---

38 *'Alternative' Ökonomie oder das Phantom in der Wissenschaft*, in "Merkur", taken from Notebook no. 500, pp. 989–993.

that only "a new way of working" would allow more vulnerable components, i.e., micro-enterprises, to enter and survive in the market, we would probably have a more balanced vision of the phenomenon that emerged in the late 1970s and early 1980s, probably not just in Europe but in North America too.

From the alternative economy to the Schumpeterian entrepreneur

Moving away from the idealistic interpretation of the "new self-employed" offered by his old colleague in the very numerous texts published in the fifteen years after the publication of Vonderach's posits, Bögenhold has increasingly applied a "Schumpeterian" interpretation to the phenomenon. Therefore, while he has continued to analyse it using sociological and anthropological categories to study the mentality of the persons in question, he has made increasing use of business economics categories that study the behaviour of enterprises and the origin of the entrepreneurial class.

The Founder's boom: myth and reality of the new self-employed was the title of the book published by Bögenhold in 1987.[39] Empirical researches conducted since the 1930s had confirmed the dual origin of self-employment, arising from the need or search

---

39   D. Bögenhold, *Der Gründerboom, Realität und Mythos der neuen Selbständigen* (Frankfurt/M-New York: Campus Verlag, 1987.

for an identity and from the lack of alternatives or desire for self-realisation. Bögenhold took a critical look at the myth of "alternative" self-employed workers, on the one hand stressing the role played by the difficult situation in the labour market, which places into context the relevance of ideological and cultural choices, and, on the other, insisting that the practice of self-employment of "alternative" enterprises is actually not very different from that of any other enterprise (*pecunia non olet*). He criticised in particular the incentive policies in favour of self-employment being pursued at that time by some public administrations in Germany to encourage non-salaried choices (*Nichtlohnarbeit*), asking the question: "In order to totally eradicate unemployment, would we like all jobless people to become self-employed workers? Is it not plain to see that a great many self-employed are finding it enormously difficult to keep their heads above water? Why delude everyone that there is room in the market when we know there isn't?" A sample survey conducted in 1985 concluded that 95% of self-employed workers in Germany had an average net monthly income a little above the bread line. Based on numerous field surveys, Bögenhold cast doubt on the *aussteigen* theory, the myth of those "getting off the capital train and devoting themselves to alternative activities". The reasons they got off the train are not worth our perusing; more than anything, they never even got on that train, and figures on graduate unemployment and the level of education of the "new" self-employed indicate that people become self-employed workers, having studied at university or not, because there is no salaried work in keeping with their level of education, and they are tired of precarious job positions. He invited his readers to take a critical view of community or cooperative solutions: it is not a spirit of "solidarity" that stimulates the birth of self-employment, but insecurity. After having demolished the image of "organic products" and "ecological" practices, Bögenhold looked at the question of the so-called *Zwitterselbständige*, i.e., non-standard workers or single-customer self-employed workers who do not have the freedom to choose their market and are not afforded the protection guaranteed to salaried workers, taking examples from the sectors of farming, construction and transport, in particular small river navigation owners. The final part of the book is devoted to a criticism of the Silicon Valley myth, one that served to stylize another ideal type figure, that of "high tech" self-employed workers, for the growth of whom relevant resources are set aside for postgraduate studies, in the form of incubators, technology parks, and so on. After having explained why the Silicon Valley model is difficult to transfer to the German situation, Bögenhold reviewed the cases of technology parks that have produced very disappointing results in terms of the creation of small high-tech firms.

The invitation to remove from the image of unsalaried work the ideological veils in which it was wrapped (those of the "alternative economy" and of a "computer-based future") was a serious appeal to having a realistic vision of self-employment and adopting an analytical method that western culture has applied to the phenomenon of employment in the capitalist age, be it salaried or unsalaried.

In a 1989 essay reviewing statistical researches on the provenance of the new self-employed, Bögenhold noted that the percentage of those coming from the jobless population had risen steadily since 1980, while a case study conducted on a significant sample of blue- and white-collar workers of a heavy engineering company, closed as a result of the crisis in the shipbuilding industry, had shown that three quarters of those that had embarked on an independent business were white-collar workers (engineers, technicians), and only a quarter were from the factory. One of the conditions deemed to be most important by interviewees in entering the new activity and the market was the "system of personal relations". It is interesting to note, too, that all interviewees said they had founded a firm, not chosen self-employment.[40]

On the basis of other empirical materials, it might be concluded that while the dominant "logic" leading to the creation of independent micro-enterprises appears to be the need to find a job ("poor" self-employment) and the possibility of offering one's specialist knowledge to the market ("rich" self-employment), the reality is that there are many other motivations and

---

40 D. Bögenhold, 'Die Berufspassage in das Unternehmertum. Theoretische und empirische Befunde zum sozialen Prozess von Firmengründungen', *Zeitschrift für Soziologie* (august 1989), 263–281.

nuances. Resuming this topic in an article for a Marxist journal[41] and recalling the debate from the 1920s, Bögenhold stressed that it was necessary to distinguish a "need economy" from a "self-realisation economy". In some periods of high unemployment, the number of self-employed grows, but the opposite can happen, too. A positive correlation exists only for the creation of the smallest size of firm and for those activities in which physical exertion is required. This is the type of self-employed worker that has no other choice, for whom German sociologists have coined the term *Existenzgründer*, literally "founder of an existence", to distinguish him from *Firmengründer*, "founder of an enterprise". One year later, when commenting on a comparative research project on ten OECD countries, Bögenhold noted that, if one takes 1950 as a benchmark, the unemployment curve and that of the incidence of self-employed workers out of all workers appear to follow the same trends until the start of the 1980s.[42] Looking at the question of self-employment based on specialist knowledge, including the liberal professions, he again observed that the considerable increase in the 1970s and 80s "was the consequence not of indigenous development but of changes going

---

41   D. Bögenhold, 'Deproletarisierung. Die Arbeitslose als Reservearmee des Unternehmertums?', *Probleme des Klassenkampfes*, 77 (1989), 75–91.

42   D. Bögenhold, 'Selbständigkeit als ein Reflex auf Arbeitslosigkeit', *Kölner Zeitschrift für Soziologie und Sozialpsychologie*, 2 (1990), 265–279.

on in white-collar work and the services sector", in particular in the areas of sanitation and healthcare, the media and publishing.[43] In a 1987 essay, taking into consideration the long cycle of postwar employment (1950–1985), he noted that the percentage of self-employed out of all workers fell continuously until 1980, before beginning to rise. The novelty was the growing number of university-educated people entering the sector, motivated by the difficulty in finding a salaried job. Moving on to figures regarding the birth and death rates of enterprises, he noted that micro-enterprises of self-employed workers were more unstable than any other enterprise size class while, considering data on bank insolvencies, they were also those suffering from the greatest economic difficulties. With reference only to West Germany before the fall of the Berlin wall, these analyses give an important general pointer, namely that self-employment, which began to become established in the 1980s, covers a vast area that encompasses both successful situations and *social hardship*.[44]

---

43 D. Bögenhold, 'Professionalisierungs – und Deprofessionalisierungstendenzen im Widerstreit. Die freien Berufe in den Dienstleistungsmärkten', in the tome ed. by Littek, Heisig and Gondek, *Dienstleistungsarbeit. Strukturveränderungen, Beschäftigungsbedingungen und Interessenlagen* (Berlin: Sigma, 1991), pp. 95–112.

44 D. Bögenhold, 'Selbständige im Beschäftigungssystem', published in the special issue of *Soziale Welt*, dedicated to the subject of "education and employment" (Göttingen 1987), 318–333.

The fall of the Berlin wall, and the great impact this event had on the cultural climate in Europe, with a veritable explosion of independent activities in the territories of the former GDR and Eastern European countries, could do no other than leave an indelible mark on thoughts about self-employment. Although it was a reworking of previous texts, Bögenhold's book published in 1994 in collaboration with Udo Staber, *Von Dämonen zu Demiurgen?*, reveals this change in the cultural climate.[45] Whereas in previous writings, in which he observed the temporal series from the end of World War II onwards and favoured the hypothesis of the progressive drop in self-employment numbers in OECD countries, with this trend slowing down in the mid-1980s, and expressed concern regarding the over-emphasis on the role of self-employment, in this text he preferred to go to Schumpeter's theory of "creative destruction": if micro-enterprises are destroyed, others are being created all the time. The core of the problem lies in the evolution and transformation of the services sector. The best usable statistical data from the EEC and Germany offer a picture of self-employment in Germany in the early 1990s that is very different from that encountered in Bögenhold's previous reflections. In previous works, perhaps influenced by Geiger's analyses on "proletaroids", he had pictured self-employment as being close to the poverty line, swaying

---

45   D. Bögenhold, U. Staber, *Von Dämonen zu Demiurgen? Zu (Re-) Organisation des Unternehmertums in Marktwirtschaften* (Berlin: Akademie Verlag, 1994).

between precarious employment and unemployment. Based on the 1991 census, he was able to assert that 48.8% of German self-employed workers had incomes in excess of 3,000-4,000 marks a month, with a vast majority of men in the group above 4,000 marks, while in lower income classes (600-3,000 marks), women were clearly more numerous. The phenomenon of self-employment was thus a structural phenomenon, and so it was possible to attempt to identify the economic laws of self-employment. The positive correlation between high unemployment/recession and the rise in self-employment, with special reference to cooperatives and partnerships, could not be completely confirmed, yet a number of elements made it likely that the role of policies to incentivise and support self-employment in countries having very different institutions, such as Germany and Great Britain, had been an important factor. Nevertheless, while the path to building a "self-employment macroeconomy" is full of difficulties, it is easier to establish the importance of relational systems, solidarity and support networks, a taking root within a social context, in accordance with the approach adopted by Granovetter.[46]

46   Mark Granovetter, 'Economic Action and Social Structure: the Problem of Embeddedness', *American Journal of Sociology*, 91 (1985), 481–510.

The end of the socialist regimes: the crisis of salaried employment deepens

It is almost as if history was getting its own back: those countries in which the salaried workers' status has represented the general form of citizenship became in the 1990s a sort of giant incubator of unsalaried work. An opportunity for assessing the effects that the fall of socialist regimes had on the status of work came in November 1992 at the international congress in Nimega, which may be considered as the first meeting of sociology researchers on second-generation self-employment.[47]

It was an important opportunity to review the state-of-the-art knowledge and theories regarding the phenomenon of self-employment, particularly in former socialist countries following the fall of the Berlin wall. Even among the so-called "international scientific community", the term "self-employment" was taking on relevance as a socio-economic category separate from "micro-enterprise".

Two main thoughts were emerging at the time, one that viewed small and micro-enterprises as a new form of development of both capitalism and democracy, a modern-day version of capitalist "animal spirits", and

---

47 *Autonomy and independent work? Experiences with restructuring industrial organization in West and East*, Nimega, 30 November-1December 1992; the conference was chaired by American sociologist Charles Sabel, co-author of the book *The Second Industrial Divide* (1984), one of the key texts for defining the Postfordist model.

another that highlighted the large gap between business organisation and self-employment, emphasising the work performed and placing it within the framework of the crisis of the capitalist model, of deindustrialisation and social malaise. Many interesting points emerged among the addresses given.

Jane Wheelock, from the Social Policies Department of the University of Newcastle, presented results based on empirical research conducted on a sample of micro-enterprises in north-east England, stressing that self-employment should be considered as a way out for those driven from production processes, and put forward four micro-enterprise configurations: subcontract, self-employment, freelance and associate employees, all operating in the "cracks" of the competitive economy, based on the intensity of work exertion, and reaching income levels close to the bread line, often below those recorded before the establishment of the micro-enterprise. Referring to researches conducted in the period between the two world wars, Wheelock argued that the family unit was the key element in the functioning of the business. The family allows for teamwork (similar to group work in the factory) and is the real driving force behind flexibility. It is one of the cornerstones of self-exploitation, being able to combine both revenue-based and emotional motivations, and is the connection between paid work and unpaid domestic work, allowing the interchange of roles between the genders, enabling the micro-enterprise to survive in the absence of public services providing support. The author recalled the concept of domestication, the use of the domestic space as a shelter against the difficulties of the market.[48]

A Bulgarian researcher, Kiril Todorov, told attendees that in his country around 180,000 new enterprises had been created between 1989 and 1992, and that the average number of workers per enterprise was a little over 3. Only 19.4% produced intangible assets, and 25% were concentrated in the area of commerce. He added that the new micro-enterprise had been a mandatory choice for those who had lost their jobs due to the dismantling of state industry. With consumer prices rising four-fold and enterprises dependent on state firms for their supplies, the new micro-enterprises were mostly formed by persons aged between 35 and 40 having a high level of education and considerable professional knowledge.[49]

---

48 J. Wheelock, 'Autonomy and dependence: the flexibility of the small business family in a peripheral local economy'. A historical reconstruction of the period between the two world wars comes in J. Foreman-Peck, 'Feed corn or chaff? New firm formation and the performance of the interwar economy', published in *Economic History Review*, 38, 3 (1985). The most interesting discussions on some aspects of self-employment in the volume edited by R. Keat and N. Abercrombie, *Enterprise Culture* (London: Routledge, 1991), are in particular the contributions of P. Bagguley, 'Postfordism and Enterprise Culture: flexibility, autonomy and changes in economic organization' and H. Rainbird, 'The self-employed: small entrepreneurs or disguised wage labourers'.

49 Kiril Todorov, *Between the entrepreneurial phase and growth phase: the challenges for the Bulgarian entrepreneur*, unpublished.

An address given by a Hungarian scholar, Klara Foti, clearly showed the interest in the Italian model of industrial districts of contemporary economists in Eastern European countries for whom, paradoxically, the terms Fordism or Fordist system of mass production were the equivalent of Soviet system, i.e., a form of production identified with state centralisation of means of production. The model of flexible specialisation has thus been for them a new paradigm of development that is not only productive but also social and democratic. Looking at the trends of a set of Hungarian manufacturing firms in the period starting with the first reforms (1968–1988), Foti showed that the drive towards competitiveness and efficiency, within the framework of an alleged independence of business decisions, was frustrated by continuous state intervention regarding product and process choices.[50]

The process of transition towards a market economy followed the template of reforms in the Communist period, with privatisation being steered from above. The state, it was argued, sold its most efficient companies to foreign groups and created, in the remaining privatised firms, tax conditions conducive to turning them into contracting enterprises.

Polish economist, Jakobik, gave a brilliant analysis, presenting a criticism of the shock therapy to which the Polish economy was subjected from 1987–88 onwards based on monetarist strategies. He laid bare

---

50   Klara Foti, *Experiences of some Hungarian enterprises. Lessons for industrial restructuring,* unpublished.

the concrete example of a "creative destruction" strategy and outlined the reasons for its failure. It was, he argued, a process to create an intentional recession to get less competitive enterprises to close, thus favouring the shift of resources towards more efficient sectors and enterprises. The plan was an undoubted success in terms of stabilising the exchange rate, cutting inflation and having more goods on the market, yet the goal of modernising the productive system was not successful. The state, adopting monetary and budgetary measures, had determined the macroeconomic situation, affecting conditions for the funding of private and public companies. There would, therefore, have been a dramatic fall in output without new initiatives, as the state did not have a strategy or industrial policy tools to act selectively and get construction under way after a period of destruction. Jakobik did not appear to believe in the models of flexible specialisation and the myth of spontaneously forming small enterprises; rather, he was in favour of mixed shareholder bases, more suitable for a take-off phase.[51]

Briton Al Rainnie expressed a similar level of scepticism regarding the fate of small enterprises and the flexible specialisation model, following on from initial studies conducted by researchers such as Bennett

---

51 Witold Jakobik, *The public enterprise in transition: towards efficiency and competition. The Polish case*, unpublished.

Harrison and Ash Amin.[52] Their idea was that modern-day capitalism is not going towards de-verticalisation, but rather towards the financial concentration of control, maintaining a network-based operating set-up in which hierarchies take on a number of forms, not just the pyramid type. Rainnie in particular observed the changes going on in contracting firms as a result of this process. He identified three types of subcontracting: that due to a lack of productive capacities, specialist contracting leading to a partnership with the client, and that of supplier. The introduction of just in time and quality control techniques was believed to have radically altered the nature of relations between the client and the subcontractor along the subcontracting chain. With the removal of "first class" enterprises, fewer and fewer in number, and moving down the chain of subcontractors, there are hierarchical relations that point to the disappearance of small independent enterprises. The lower — or the more peripheral (in terms of functions, not territory) — one goes, the more subcontractors become interchangeable. Large enterprises will search for those having the lowest labour costs. It is very

---

52 Al Rainnie, *Subcontracting and the global, local connection. Myth and reality.* The text expressly referred to by Rainnie is B. Harrison and M. Kelley, *Outsourcing and the search for flexibility*, Working Paper 90/14, of the School of Urban and Public Affairs of Carnegie Mellon University, 1990. Of Ash Amin's researches we refer in particular to A. Amin and M. Dietrich, *From hierarchy to hierarchy*, an address presented to the European Association for Evolutionary Political Economy, 1990.

illusory to think one can found local economies on such a fragile base and on such despotic relations with the client. Clients, i.e., large enterprises, will resort more and more to outsourcing and to global sourcing; for a time they will use subcontractors found locally before making use of subcontractors located elsewhere. He thus argued that the "Post-Fordist" model was in decline, no longer representing the new economy. This also marked the decline of "localisms". A Swiss researcher thought differently and, based on a case study on clock production in Jura, argued that thanks to the presence of local sub-cultures, local economies are better able to stand apart from the colonisation of patterns of thinking, and thus to develop successful innovation in the market.

Of considerable interest was the study presented by Russians Natalia Chernina and Efim Chernin, in which a clear distinction was made between small enterprises and self-employment, and ideological prejudice in favour of or against the Post-Fordist model was absent. According to the two Russian researchers, small enterprises, born out of the independence of units that break away from large enterprises or privatised in the form of an equity participation of workers, are a dynamic force in the Russian economy and labour market, yet they have not been responsible for innovative processes, for three basic reasons: i) the tendency of new shareholders to allocate dividends rather than invest profits in new machinery; ii) the absence of support from universities in the areas of training and research, being totally oblivious to the world of small business, and dependent on the military-

96

industrial complex, and iii) the coincidence of the take-off phase and onset of the economic crisis.[53]

Nevertheless, even after the Nimega congress, it appeared clear that the research world had a problem separating self-employment from enterprise, and preferred to use the English term of business which, being a generic term for profit-oriented working activity, covers all bases. It was already a step forward that the organisers of the event preferred to use the word work instead of business in the title of the event.

The former GDR territories as a laboratory for self-employment

Following the collapse of the East German regime (German Democratic Republic, GDR), the *Länder* of the East underwent a very radical process of deindustrialisation. In a few years, millions of salaried jobs were lost, not only in industry but more generally in all public sector companies, in both the services and agricultural sectors, which had been established in the regime as "enterprises belonging to the people" (*volkseigene Betriebe*). Many party officials and members of the state apparatus were also out of a job and a wage, from university lecturers to army officers. As self-employment had been reduced to a minor role,

---

53   N. Chernina e E. Chernin, *The potential of small business in solving socio-economic problems of Russia during transition to a market economy*, unpublished.

being identified with the "private" sector, the fall of the Honecker regime gave rise to one of the biggest catastrophes of salaried employment in modern-day history. It is thus natural for the community present in the eastern *Länder* of modern-day Germany to end up becoming an enormous self-employment laboratory, given its inability to survive with only aid and transfers from western *Länder*, the Bund and the European Union, and with efforts to convert production capacity creating few jobs. Here we should be talking about *Selbständige dritter Generation*, or "third generation" independent workers, their traits being very different from those of the "alternative" workers of the 1970s. The dynamics by virtue of which they have been forced to attempt the path of self-employment are different: mostly unwanted, but endured, coming within the framework of *Ökonomie der Not*, the need economy, and in that of self-realisation. They have also suffered a trauma, passing from a society in which work time was very slow to a society in which work time is frenetic, from a society that guaranteed a home, education, a minimum work income and pension to a society that offers many fewer guarantees. Whereas the cultural background and subjectivity of the "new self-employed" of the 1970s appeared to be appropriate for the promotion of self-employment, the opposite may be said for citizens from the former GDR. The socialist regime was, however, partly able to give them valuable "human capital", which many were able to use in the self-employment market: a high quality compulsory school education, often better than that given to children in the junior and high schools of the western world.

Michael Thomas of the Berlin Institute for socioeconomic studies is one of the leading researchers of self-employment in the territories of the former GDR. In a 1993 article in "Soziale Welt", he warned against overly optimistic visions of the phenomenon. In the final years of the GDR, craft firms were in steady decline. After 1989, there was a boom in new enterprises (15,604 in the first four months of 1990 and 85,826 in the final four months of that year, with 1,200 new businesses a day being set up in July and August, just prior to monetary union). In 1991 there were on average 60,000 new enterprises being founded every four months; in 1992 the figure was about 50,000. However, operating conditions for an independent business were difficult due to the general economic situation and, for example, the hike in rents for business premises. It may have been a flash in the pan — only the future will tell — yet the phenomenon was important as a general social reawakening, a "genesis of the actors" with a new form of protagonism and changes to the anthropology of work.[54]

Other research, conducted in the region of Berlin in the period September 1992-August 1995 by a working group on the "new self-employed" headed by Thomas, calculated that there were around 500,000 owners of new enterprises in the territories of the former GDR at the end of 1995. This figure included immigrant Germans from

---

54   V.M. Thomas, 'Private Selbständigkeit in Ostdeutschland — Erste Schritte in einem neuen Forschungsfeld', *Soziale Welt*, 2 (1993), 225–242, and the rich bibliography provided therein.

the West, foreign nationals, and expat GDR citizens who had returned home. Almost 70% of these owners came from the previous status of "white-collar worker". There were low percentages for jobless, low-skilled workers and aid beneficiaries. The death rate of enterprises was, however, extremely high: above 50%. The voting trends of the new self-employed at the 1994 general elections were interesting: 45.4% voted for CDU, 21% for SPD, 15% for PDS, 7.2% for Greens/Democratic alliance. The situation was different only for the district of Berlin (direct 1995 survey): 27.9% voted for CDU, 20.9% for PDS, 18.6% for Greens/Democratic alliance, 16.3% for SPD. Interestingly, a relevant percentage of self-employed workers were elected among the officials and administrators of the new parties. In the Berlin region in 1995, the highest percentage of these were from the PDS, the Communist refoundation party. The participation of men and women was surprising: in Berlin-Brandenburg in 1995, 72.1% were men, just 27.9% women. Also noteworthy was the almost non-existent affiliation to business or trade union organisations, bearing out the "gap in representation" of self-employment.[55]

Translation by Paul Warrington

---

55 Final research project, Berlin, December 1995, M. Thomas (project supervisor), T. Koch, G. Valerius, R. Woderich, *Neue Selbständige im Transformationsprozess: Herkunftswege, soziale Charakteristika und Potentiale*, Technische Universität Magdeburg; project financed by Volkswagen Foundation.

TEN PARAMETERS
FOR DEFINING THE STATUS
OF SELF-EMPLOYED WORKERS

The status of salaried (dependent) work is now fully recognized in society and has been drafted and set down in law, while that of self-employed workers still has to be created. By status I mean not only an accurate definition of self-employed workers' traits and modes of existence, giving them a social-type figure clearly separate from that of other figures, but also a means to recognise it. By statute, I mean a legally defined social condition.

In order to draw up a self-employed workers' status, it is necessary to single out the constituent parts of work and the basic underlying social relations.

I have selected ten parameters (content, perception of space, perception of time, professional identity, form of remuneration, resources needed to enter the market, resources needed to stay in the market, the market, organisation and representation of interests, citizenship) that can form the basis for constructing a self-employed workers' status. These parameters might also be seen as ten key variables for constructing an *economic policy* for *self-employment*.

So let us begin with the first parameter, that concerning the *content* of self-employment. It is evident from the review of studies referred to in the preceding essay that self-employment can be a form of work requiring a high degree of technical and scientific knowledge, or a high degree of physical exertion: both high- and low-skilled work, intellectual and manual. Between these two extremes we have a full range of work content characteristics. This is no different from salaried work.

The content of work is, however, different if one considers the degree of prescription inherent in the organisation. Work may be manual, low-skilled, with a high degree of physical exertion, but it changes radically in terms of content if it is performed under a Taylorist regime, in which times and methods are assigned from above, or if there is no prescription from above. The predetermined movements of a worker on the assembly line, within a well-defined socio-technical space, do not require planning for necessary resources and the way they will be deployed as much as the set of basic movements and tasks required of a self-employed worker, moving in a socio-technical space that is not predetermined. The degree of non-prescription gives the self-employed worker responsibility for planning that is at odds with the logic of repetitiveness and manual skills, and tends to centre on the assessment and allocation of resources, thus on the knowledge — experiential and theoretical — needed to attain the greatest productivity from the combination of basic tasks and unforeseeable situations. Work with a high knowledge content supplied under a salaried work regime will always be framed within a method that prescribes the use of knowledge broken down into a series of disciplines, and a process that resorts to formalised knowledge. The same type of work performed as a self-employed worker leaves room for the use of knowledge outside the formalised framework, a customised combination of information taken from a broad "basket" of knowledge. As this "basket" of knowledge is customised, with many possible combinations, work content will be different even if the work performed is the same.

Yet what makes self-employment fundamentally different from salaried employment is the content of requirements in terms of *relations and communication*. As such tasks are deemed, in the world of wage-earners, not to be value-adding, but simply as additional costs of self-employment, they are not entered in the "budget" of the work performed. They are a cost charged to the work provider, and not an extra value of his work. It appears indeed that relational and communication work cannot be gauged otherwise in the individual exchange between the recipient and supplier of the work/service. Relational work, viewed as an additional unit of required work, multiplied by the number of persons performing it, has ended up becoming a new market (expanding the existing communication market, or in the form of new communication segments/markets) and forming the basis of a relational work *culture*, the traits of which have never been examined. Just like domestic work performed by women which, before the feminist movement, was socially invisible, not entered in the "budget" of society, and thus considered as non-work, so relational work performed by self-employed workers is invisible, not entered in the budget of society and not considered as work content.

Self-employment will never be a fully-fledged citizen in the labour market as long as its relational elements continue to be viewed as an *external diseconomy of Postfordism*. Self-employment will not be able to have a statute separate from that of salaried work as long as the creation of a new market of relations is not recognised as an extra resource of the Postfordist system, as long as *relational work* is not recognised as the distinguishing feature of a *Zivilisation* different from those coming before it. Here we might refer to the observations of other economists and sociologists that consider communication to be a commodity.

How many hours of the day does a self-employed worker devote to "relations"? Many have expressed the large amount of time spent performing relational work out of the number of hours worked during the day with the phrase "I spend a lot of time on the phone".

Reasoning by analogy with salaried work, it might be said that the high incidence of relational work is an *unproductive* component of the working day of the self-employed worker, a cost deriving from the breakup of the enterprise organisation, obliging the self-employed worker to go and retrieve in space the *scattered fragments* of the Taylorist enterprise. In order to establish a self-employed workers' statute, we have to abandon this old way of reasoning. The implosion of the large enterprise should be seen as a "creative destruction", the liberation of a new social need, the creation of the relational work market, the source of a new skill, thus a "resource" that the self-employed worker can get hold of in order to establish his independence from the client and from work in general. The daily obligation of forging links, the extra unrecognised work considered to be a limitation, labour that is non-marketable in the current stage of development of Postfordist production, in short unpaid work, may instead be seen — if the self-employed worker is fully aware of his status — as an opportunity to be grasped, within the context of new independence and the identification of new negotiating spaces, which can serve to diminish the current status of relational work as unpaid work.

Once the relevance of relational work in his working day has been recognised, the independent worker may be able to better gauge the *services* that can be of assistance to him in performing relational work with lower costs, the *knowledge* that can serve to carry out relational work in a more sophisticated manner, the *social horizons* that may open up so that what was previously an obligation can become a springboard for greater autonomy, for his new social recognition the negotiating space that can open up with public and private actors that obtain an economic or social advantage from the growth of the culture of relational work. There will then come a time when the independent worker recaptures the *surplus* generated by his unpaid relational work.

The perception of space

Second-generation self-employment has acquired its own specificity in the period from the 1970s to today. It finds itself at a point in time in which the organisation of space shaped by Taylorism, in both factories and offices, has been unravelling. The perception of space on the part of the salaried worker referred to two clearly separated "places", two separate systems of rules and cultures: home and the factory; home and the office; the domain of private life, of the family, of affections, and the domain of work. The primary characteristic of self-employment is the *domestication* of the workplace, the assimilation of work within the set of rules of private life, even when the two spaces — home and work — are kept separate. Work does not have to be performed at home or with the assistance of family members for it to be a form of *domestication*. The workplace simply has to be conceived as a place where the rules are established by the independent worker, such that the culture and habits of one's private life are transferred to the workplace. The first consequence of this is that working hours mirror the habits and life cycles of private life. The second consequence is a change in mental habits in relation to the various coordinates of civic life. Compared with the salaried worker, who was accustomed to spending most of his active life in a space that was not his but belonged to others, which others had shaped and organised, and where others had written down the rules to be followed in that space, the self-employed worker has developed a greater sense of "ownership" of the established rules in spaces, and is thus less willing to accept other people's rules. While the "alienation" of paid work divided the individual's life into two socio-emotional cycles, one's private life and working life, the (apparent) non-alienation of self-employment reduces one's existence to a single socio-emotional cycle, that of the private sphere.

Industrial districts constitute a particular form of working space organisation, in which there coexist different types of functional relations, through which space is structured: the traditional enterprise, in which most work is salaried, and the independent micro-enterprise. Both types, however, are present in a single local space, in a single territory, in which the place for working and place for living overlap and eventually combine. Within such a district, the place for living has characteristics that are different from a *company town*. In the Fordist "factory village" the rules of work were imposed on domestic rules, and from an urban planning and architectural point of view the factory model was reproduced in the housing model. In industrial districts, on the other hand, it appears that the interpenetration of workplace and habitation has produced a "third set of rules", a hybrid model, a sort of "residential territory of production", which, while no longer having any real influence on the urban and architectural modelling of space (making wasteful use of the territory, building without planning), has nevertheless brought about forms of social cohesion, and given structure to cooperative social relations (osmosis of innovative processes, endogenous training of the workforce) in forms that are closer to the mentality of the self-employed worker than that of the employee.

To demonstrate how important the elimination of the separation between home and work is for the definition of a self-employment statute, one simply has to consider the attempts being made by the capitalist system to "salarize" self-employment. A first example refers to teleworking.

As the capitalist system has realised that the *domestication* of work can raise productivity and relieve the worker from the anxiety of feeling "alienated", that home-to-office mobility may have a heavy social cost and become a cost for the enterprise, it now looks favourably on forms of employment, such as telework, which make it possible to reconcile the place of living with the place of work. Yet as soon as it came into being, telework highlighted the difficulty in setting new rules for salaried employment performed in the worker's home. As far as self-employment is concerned, there are no problems regarding privacy, since the place of work is the same as the place of living. With regard to salaried work, which by definition belongs to "others", it is necessary to create a new set of rules in order to re-separate what telework sought to unite, with the difficult goal of retracing, in a limited and mono-functional place, such as a normal apartment, the boundaries between the private sphere of rights and the sphere of rights shared with the employer. Another possible solution is that of building "asylums" of teleworkers, commercial buildings set aside solely for their use. This would take us back to the situation already in place, i.e. the home-office binary system typical of salaried work.

The second example pertains to the networked enterprise, i.e. an enterprise with an organisation that consists of several coordinated workplaces. The Marshallian definition of an industrial district was that of a *factory without walls* spread over the territory. Coordination between the dominant firm and subcontracting firms, many operating under a form of self-employment, has ensured extraordinary flexibility for a long time, but has also highlighted the high costs involved in work to coordinate and physically exchange goods and services between the dominant firm and its network of subcontractors. As long as these costs were passed on to the collective or the subcontractor, things could continue as before, but with the emergence of pressing technical and organisational constraints threatening to make the system ungovernable (e.g., during the road hauliers' strike), the idea was raised of bringing single subcontractors back within the *walls* of the dominant enterprise, based on the concept of an "*intra muros*" network.

But whatever might be imagined in terms of returning to the Tayloristic organisation of working space, it will not be possible to erase the new frame of mind of the self-employed, resulting from the overlapping of the domestic, socio-emotional sphere and the sphere of work.

The *domestication* of work is a condition of modern man, and it is up to him to use it to attain greater freedom or undergo greater slavery. There is no doubt, however, that it forms part of the elements of self-employment, and as such is one of the factors making up its specific constitution.

The perception of time

There is no other element making up the self-employment constitution as specific as the sense of time. It might be said that the basic difference between salaried and self-employed work is the different organisation of work time. An employee's work time is regulated, that of the independent work is rule-free, thus limitless. The only common theme running through the history of the regulation of work time from the industrial revolution to the present day has been the fixing of time limits to salaried work, the unit of measurement being the working day or working week. The history of industrial salaried work as a social movement, as a coalition in defence of class interests, has advanced in line with that of the regulation of work time. Indeed, the holiday celebrating salaried work, May 1st, is the day that commemorates the sacrifice made by workers as they fought to limit the working day to eight hours.

Despite this epochal change, the consequent lengthening of the working day not only appears to have gone unnoticed: illustrious sociologists and essayists, who love to analyse modern-day capitalism, are actually saying quite the opposite, that work time is going down. To understand this paradox we should firstly consider the effects that the "automation myth" has had on the analysis of modern-day capitalism and then consider the structure of employment statistics in single European countries, including those in the European Union and the OECD.

By "automation myth" I mean the belief that the replacement of the workforce with machinery controlled by artificial intelligence, in terms of manual tasks and highly complex intellectual tasks, would lead to an era of contentment, of "freedom from work", and there would be an increase in the amount of leisure time available to citizens. To substantiate this belief, sets of statistics are produced, demonstrating that since the last century working hours have gradually decreased. While it is undoubtedly true that, over the long term, working hours have tended to decrease in industrially advanced countries — a tangible sign of trade union action in the sphere of salaried work — it is also true that employment statistics, from the 1930s onwards, have not changed radically in terms of approach, and continued to be produced in the same way even when, after the 1970s, the structure of employment altered radically with the burgeoning areas of self-employment and unregulated and precarious labour in the "poor" tertiary sector. Employment statistics are based chiefly on "strong" contractual areas of salaried work, in particular the working hours of sectors marked by the presence of large private enterprises and public employment sectors, and consider to a lesser extent the area of small and medium enterprises, as well as the situation in "poor" tertiary sectors that are not protected by the unions and *do not take into account* self-employed working hours. The more the employment pyramid base is broadened the more the representation of work time becomes distorted. To find a way out of this absurd situation, in 1987 the European Union introduced a direct survey (introduced by Italy only in 1992), which has evident limitations but has been sufficient to throw some light onto the reality of the working times of self-employed workers, and to dismiss the belief about freedom from work and an increase in workers' leisure time. To understand how reality has been deformed by statistics, we can cite an example that many can relate to.

Let us imagine we have to give a statistical evaluation, using current criteria, of average weekly working hours in the freight transport sector. This evaluation will take into account the contractual hours worked by workers employed with "transport" contracts (the workers of shipping companies and couriers, railway and airline workers, port workers and seafarers), together with the average amount of overtime worked in the week or month. The calculation will not include self-employed workers, for instance independent road hauliers, who make up the vast majority of workers in this sector, and work an average of 60-65 hours a week, or cooperatives of forklift operators, which make up the vast majority of the manual workforce in warehouses and freight centres. If we think that only the minority of Italian shipping companies and couriers are big enough to have a contractual system controlled by trade unions, it is easy to see that the working hours of shipping company workers, taken as a baseline by official statistics, is a very vague indicator of working hours actually worked in the sector. It appears indeed that only the contractual working hours of airline and railway workers are able to mirror the reality of working hours in the respective sectors. But those who know anything about the sector are aware that this section of the workforce makes up only a small percentage of the whole freight transport sector. What is more, only a fraction of the workforce responsible for freight transport in the railway and air transport segments is governed by national contracts, with the growth of cooperatives, or self-employed workers, or employees of enterprises whose employment contracts are not based on the "transport" sector. The biggest problem in sectors that are changing rapidly, such as freight transport and third party logistics, is the fact that contractual relations bear no real relation to the way work is actually organised. Let us look at the rapidly expanding sector of so-called "third party logistics providers" with the respective freight storage, processing and distribution centres. In Italy there is no single labour contract for workers in this sector, and each enterprise acts independently, resorting to contracts from different sectors: commerce, industry, shipping, general stores, or special group contracts. The majority of these enterprises and the work they do are not classified under the item "transport"; moreover, the payroll of these enterprises is only partly formed by salaried employees (often less than 50% of the total), the remainder being members of cooperatives or independent workers. But that is not all. If we take the trouble to read the more recent contracts, we see that in the 1990s there was a radical transformation of the organisation of work formalised at a contractual level. The structure of the employee's timetable under an open-ended contract is such that, even though he is guaranteed a weekly timetable of 38 hours, the system of flexibility in place for working hours, with shifts going around the clock all day, seven days a week and 363 days a year (the only holidays being 1 May and 25 December) means that hours worked are actually 30-40% longer.

In short, the image that statistics offer of the working day is quite a distorted one, even when we consider salaried workers, and statistics for the hours of non-salaried workers are either unreliable or absent. If a job of six hours a day can be considered as *part-time* work, it means that something has changed in the working day.

Having spelled out, hopefully clearly, the complex calculations involved in reckoning working hours in a Postfordist world, let us return to the hours worked by self-employed persons.

In addition to *domestication*, the other factor that causes self-employed workers to have longer working day is the form of remuneration, which is no longer commensurate with elementary units of time (hour, month), but with the performance of work for which only the result counts, often generically, namely the product of said work and meeting of the delivery deadline. And for the same product, should the client request a closer deadline (with or without an increase in remuneration) the working day of the self-employed worker will be affected by "time cutting" — visible and documentable in the Fordist factory, invisible in the sphere of self-employment.

Another factor that contributes to longer working days are the so-called "unwritten market rules", by which if a self-employed worker does not accept the requested delivery conditions, he "exits the market", i.e. a sort of temporary dismissal that will enable him to reflect on his weak contractual position and, in most cases, force him to go back to the client, head bowed, ready to sell himself at a lower price.

More intense work rates may also be caused by the desire for higher earnings, an opportunity available to the self-employed worker but not to the salaried worker. The way in which self-employed workers manage to handle these constraints — personal sacrifices, inventiveness, tricks — forms part of the "invisible history of work" that one day a historian might be able to reconstruct based on oral sources and the few available documents, as has happened for the history of paid work.

"Widespread reduction in working hours", "working less means work for all": these slogans are hollow rhetoric for Postfordist salaried work, never mind self-employment. Nevertheless, they express a widely felt thought and refer to civilised values. Until self-employed workers have found their own original forms of self-protection, there is the risk that any new rights introduced by the legislator will remain just words on paper or be entrusted solely to the discipline of the judiciary.

An unlimited working day is not the only difference in the perception of working time between employees and self-employed workers. A second difference relates to the perception of time within one's life plans. The immanent risk of failure is part of the self-employment constitution: the feeling of walking on a tightrope, the possibility of going quickly from middle-class well-being to abject poverty, the so-called "poverty risk" of self-employed workers. These produce a psycho-social frame of mind that makes long-term planning impossible. Many things can go wrong: an accident that sidelines the worker for six months, a big invoice that is not paid, a damages claim from a client, the bankruptcy, wilful or otherwise, of a supplier or client, which can lead to rack and ruin for the worker and his collaborators. The sense of insecurity caused by market mechanisms and the complete absence of economic "shock absorbers" leads the self-employed worker to seek "insurance" in the form of a greater accumulation of wealth. Self-employment is also closely tied up with family destinies, and many imbalances can be caused by generational choices or behaviour. The refusal of children, for example the sons and daughters of craftsmen, to follow in their father's or mother's footsteps leads not only to the loss of a lifetime of expertise and professional skills, but also to an intensification of efforts in the short term, with the worker believing that time is "short", being incapable of "thinking big" or being innovative.

It would, however, be misleading to characterise the perception of the work time of a self-employed worker only in a negative manner, in terms of added exploitation and permanent insecurity. The collapse of regulated working hours and the self-organisation of work time have given to a large section of modern-day society a new sense of freedom, a new way of looking at institutions and regulating processes, moving the frontiers of democracy and imposing upon the individual the control of his existence, giving him the possibility of creating a way of life that is better than that offered by salaried work. It is, however, difficult to grasp the "collective" sense of this transformation, the ability to shape a new civilisation, for now the effects have been seen only at an individual level.

The form of remuneration

After the different perception of work time, the form of remuneration is another basic component of self-employment. For some authors, it is the most important, since the definition of *unsalaried work* is sufficient to characterise it legally and socially. This definition is used in particular by French authors, such as Gerard Lyon Caen (G. Lyon Caen, *Le droit du travail non salarié*, Ed. Sirey, Paris 1990).

There are indeed many arguments in their favour. Firstly, the importance of the wage form in the culture of industrialism and economic theory, in particular in Marxist theory. The figure of the salaried worker or wage earner was firstly seen as a kind of archetype of the subordinate social figure, and after the October Revolution in Russia and US New Deal, took on the more general meaning of "citizen" enjoying all the rights enshrined by the Welfare State. The salary/wage form is thus a product of industrialism, in particular in the Fordist phase.

If the wage form enters a crisis as a general form of remuneration in an employment relationship, a crisis ensues for the legal system built around that form. Thus the figures that are not paid with a salary or wage in an employment relationship are figures that belong to another social status, and do not come under the sphere of rights granted to dependent work.

For both 19th century liberalism and 20th century protectionism, the wage form was always associated with *guaranteeing the survival of the workforce*. With its payment schedules (daily, weekly, monthly), the salary/wage has been accepted in all stages of industrialism as an economic form, by means of which the employer guaranteed to the employee the minimum subsistence necessary to replenish the energy needed to work. When the Welfare State was established, the form of direct salary/wage was supplemented by that of indirect wage, by means of which the State guaranteed the subsistence of a worker temporarily unable to perform his job and his survival once he was no longer a salaried worker or wage-earner.

As self-employment expanded in modern-day industrialism and capitalism, the principle that the *subsistence* of the workforce is no longer a problem to be sorted out by the employer or the State first came to be accepted. This happened with the replacement of the wage form of remuneration with a different form, that of the *invoice*. There could have been no bigger revolution as regards the social status of work. While the wage was the economic form of workforce reproduction, the *non-wage form* put an instant stop to the problem of reproducing the workforce as an essential problem of social relations, and consequently of *contractual* relations between the employer and the worker, and of *citizenship* relations between the worker and the State. This was a radical shift, with the fundamental principle of *guaranteeing workers' subsistence* being replaced by the de facto condition of *existential risk*.

Guaranteeing subsistence was the objective underlying the scheduling of remuneration in the salary/wage form. For the payment times of an invoice to be compatible with the principle of ensuring the reproduction of the workforce, not only should they be well defined and agreed upon by the parties, their payment within the agreed time limit should also be guaranteed with a minimum of legal protection. Since the only legal basis for self-employment relations is to be found in the Italian legal system in some articles of the Civil Code, and since these law provisions in no way re-introduce the principle of guaranteeing the subsistence of the workforce through the form of remuneration, the attempts being made to extend to self-employed workers some of the fundamental rights of salaried work contained in the Labour Code and the

Statute of Salaried Workers are to be considered as *insufficient*. This is because they seek to re-introduce laws taken from the history and practices of the Welfare State — from that labour-based system of the 20th century — when non-salaried self-employment is still not covered by the *principle of guaranteeing the subsistence of the workforce*, which even the forms of 19th century liberal capitalism held to be necessary for ensuring the physical and mental well-being of workers.

Never mind the sphere of additional guarantees offered by the Welfare State, non-salaried workers are still waiting for some basic guarantees. Only legal protection for ensuring that clients adhere to payment times for a professional service can bring non-salaried work into the culture of securing the survival of the workforce, which even the crudest forms of 19th century liberal capitalism recognised. Here too we should remember the profound changes that have been happening in the sphere of work organisation.

Modern-day unsalaried work does not consist solely of "human capital", of the individual's physical and mental energies and knowledge, it also consists of constant capital, i.e. vehicles, machinery, equipment, which may also be extremely costly and sophisticated. Thus in order to eliminate *existential risk*, it is necessary to ensure not only the reproduction of the workforce but also the preservation of constant capital. Neither the client nor the State can completely disregard the *wealth of means of production* currently held by the self-employed. Should they do so, the country risks further economic decline. Respecting payment times for invoices is first and foremost a question of restoring a citizenship that has been denied and is only secondarily a question of the relationship between the amount of the remuneration agreed upon and delivery times.

The expansion of unsalaried work developed out of a tacit "devil's pact" between clients and work providers, both parties aware they were devaluing the authority of the welfare state. The *existential risk* was freely accepted by the self-employed worker. It is no coincidence that the generations permeated by a *no future* culture, having a desperate and short-term vision of life, were the first to be willing to undersign the non-wage pact. The story of each country is different, however, and so the status of self-employment has been perceived in different ways, giving rise to different sorts of conflict. In Italy, where in the 1990s the rise in fiscal pressure on citizens was higher than in any other industrial country, where unsalaried work plays a key role in various areas of the economy, where the quality of services provided by the public administration is often poor, there have been episodes of tax revolt that have helped to worsen the crisis of institutional legitimacy and of the national State. Those representing the culture of salaried work have risen to defend those institutions, making self-employed workers out to be subversive and tax dodgers, and re-evoking the image of a middle class that is dangerous for the democratic institutions, that were constructed back in the 1930s after Hitler came to power. The great confusion that came about has, however, helped to better clarify the traits of *second-generation non-salaried work*, i.e. specifically Postfordist self-employment, and to highlight the fact that the evasion of taxes by self-employed persons, whose activity is not part of the outsourcing of services on the part of enterprises or the public administration, can dodge taxes more easily that by those whose clients are organisations having an interest in documenting their expenditure. The invoices issued are therefore also *tax documents*.

If one reflects on what has been said above, it is possible to have a better understanding of the psycho-social change in the Postfordist present and the possible relocation of forms of political conflict and social malaise. Remuneration in the form of payment of an invoice no longer takes the form of a guarantee of workforce subsistence, but rather that of a tax payment. It marks the worker's commitment to a State that denies him some fundamental rights of citizenship. On many occasions, self-employed workers are faced with due VAT payments without having the cash needed to pay their collaborators, due to the late payments of invoices on the part of the client!

Professional identity

In a culture still governed by the salaried work statute, professional identity is the only form of recognition of self-employment. Professional identity appears to sum up the entire social status of self-employment. It is thus important to reflect on the characteristics of professional identity in the Postfordist era, starting, as we have done so far, from the other side of the coin, the Fordist era. The main trait of the normal factory worker appeared to be the *absence of professional identity*. The skill of the factory worker was that of not having any skills, being interchangeable, and willing to move in a world labour market when the concept of globalization was still a long way off. In the 1920s and 1930s there was a flowering of studies on the new middle classes and white collar workers (see the preceding essay), highlighting in particular the great demand for technical and professional knowledge from the labour market and the equally strong *depersonalisation* of professional capabilities caused by the standardisation of white-collar work. Professional competence no longer belonged to the person but to the role covered. It was only with the development of the tertiary sector and of new sectors such as the media that in the period between the two world wars there was a flourishing of new professional figures, interpreted by individuals. At the same time, however, the standardisation of training systems (vocational training and university education), combined with an education system that began to include all members of society in advanced capitalist countries, intensified the trend of "faceless professionals" suitable for the Fordist factory and large-scale organised systems. Large companies incorporated the professional skills of the individual, whose social status remained linked to his status as a salaried worker. Only the so-called "liberal professions" appeared to be immune from this depersonalisation process, but in the 1970s the reorganisation of the healthcare system and standardisation of some professional legal services began to eat away at this privilege too.

The growth and spread of self-employment in the 1970s was therefore a radical turning point in respect of Fordism, with *professionalism becoming once again a personal attribute*, having the traits typical of an individual, and of that alone. This was thus a strong reassertion of the role of the individual, of the importance of individual diversities, emerging with Postfordism: a reaffirmation that may appear to be *a cultural breakthrough* in relation to the barbarism of depersonalisation, to the seizure of one's professional identity. With the resurgence of professionalism, *craftsmanship* — the oldest form of professionalism that can also confer social status — has been rediscovered and relaunched.

The unsalaried worker, deprived of the subsistence guarantees mentioned above, is to an extent rewarded with the return of his professional identity, preserve of the large enterprise in the Fordist era. Postfordism might be seen as the outsourcing of professional identities. The large enterprise frees itself of them, then takes them back as external suppliers, retaining within it only the relative control functions. The market becomes a market offering skills rather than merits. Professional identity viewed as self-fulfilment, self-realisation, is undoubtedly a powerful impetus for creativity as well as being a frame of reference for moral principles.

Unfortunately market reality does not quite live up to this cultural ideal: those with more skills, more knowledge, better professional qualities, manage to get them acknowledged and to win that freedom that we all aspire to, the peace of mind of offering the highest level of quality in our day-to-day work.

The purchasing market increasingly views *cost* as the key component of relations with the self-employed. Those who cost less are preferred to those with greater skills. Professional identity is increasingly a commodity that cannot be exchanged, and the service provided is filled with contents other than those of competence. The "expert response" bends ever more in the direction of the customer's political needs, his power-related problems in the company or the organisation he belongs to.

In the public sector market, the patronage system is predominant. In a country such as Italy, where the mafia-like party system is pervasive, controlling huge amounts of public expenditure, the power of competence plays second fiddle to the power of clientelism.

Another great obstacle to the development of a market of professional skills of unsalaried workers is the university "corporation", which is increasingly active in the skills market with forms of unfair competition. As the amount of funding available to faculties dwindles, university lecturers go looking for resources in the skills market, making use of available office equipment paid for by the State and often unpaid labour (students, PhD students, researchers).

This is not, however, the real criticality of competition between self-employed workers and university lecturers. We can understand that our society has maintained caste-based feudal systems from the fact that the quality of a university lecturer's work is *notarised*, thus the customer will find it hard to object to, as it bears the signature of a public official, to whom the State has conferred the title of expert, while the customer is fully able to gauge the quality of the service provided by the self-employed worker.

But even when faced by these inequalities, self-employed workers should not whine about it. It may be that the impossibility of using one's skills in a market dominated by the least-cost principle, by political clientelism and by caste privileges will induce self-employed workers to invest their professional identities in innovative areas of the *non-profit* sector, allowing them to become aware of the poverty of the market and invest greater time and energy in efforts to create new rules of democracy, in which "know-how" prevails.

Resources needed to enter the market

Three key elements emerge from the researches we will be reviewing in the following essays, fundamental for being able to enter the sphere of self-employment: a) the network of acquaintances of personal, family and social knowledge and relations, b) specialist knowledge

126

possessed, c) inventiveness, i.e. creativity, ability to discover and to invest in one's aptitudes, including the positive elements of one's character. Little attention has been paid, on the other hand, to the question of financing the fixed capital required and specific lending instruments in favour of micro-enterprises.

As far as the first element is concerned, the increasingly difficult state of the labour market, which makes it very difficult for new generations to get a full-time job, does not appear to be very different from the situation of salaried work. Official labour placement systems are now acknowledged by everyone as systems that are not very good at "finding jobs". It is, however, personal and family acquaintances and networks of social and political relations that, in Europe, appear to be the main way of finding salaried employment. The self-employment constitution is, however, a little different, also with regard to the way the system of social relations works. In salaried employment, these relations serve to take the job-seeker to the doorstep of the workplace, and stop there, whereas in self-employment they continue to be crucial for the very survival of the micro-enterprise, becoming a constant element of its reproduction.

The second key element concerns the type and level of specialist knowledge of the self-employed worker. Here too, the self-employment status does not appear at first sight to differ significantly from that of salaried work. For both types of employment, we must consider the two systems of higher education and compulsory education. Researches conducted on self-employment

127

in former socialist countries, in particular the territories of former East Germany (GDR), have concluded that the better functioning of the compulsory education system is one of the factors that make self-employed workers from former socialist countries more competitive than their colleagues in the West. Since the report *Made in America* denounced the disaster of high school education in the United States, the problem of the progressive deterioration of basic education in western countries has come to light. With specialist knowledge quickly becoming obsolescent as modern technologies evolve, a sound basic education is a key factor in allowing people who are forced to move from one job to another or from one service to another to be able to adapt and relocate. Both for salaried work, which is increasingly precarious, and for self-employment, the *skill* needed to do a good job is acquired by doing that job. But the set of tools that go to form a knowledge of the learning method and the mindset with which someone tackles the questions of finding a job and integrating in society are, or should be, acquired in the period of compulsory and secondary education rather than in university and specialist education. However, the disastrous plight of state schools in many western countries and the enormous influence wielded by the media in shaping the collective mindset appear to have put an end to this chapter of the history of our civilisation. The school is becoming increasingly a question of social discipline, thus one of law and order. The way things are going, the ministry of the interior will be taking over the running of schools. From this point of view, the resources needed to enter self-employment and the problems involved in obtaining them do not appear to be different from salaried work. There are, however, differences that are not such as to create a diversity of constitution.

The situation changes if we view self-employment as both a job and an enterprise. In this case, there is a radical difference compared with salaried work. Ever since the 19th century, economic sociologists have considered access to credit as being a key condition for creating the social figure of entrepreneur, and the credit institution as a prerequisite for the existence of the enterprise. As far as self-employment is concerned, forms of credit aimed at micro-enterprises have only been developed, in Italy and overseas, in the craft sector. Leasing may be considered a form of financing dedicated to self-employed workers. Generally speaking, however, the banking system is not a service that the self-employed worker can resort to, and the profit levels posted by micro-enterprises are never going to attract financial investments. The production of cash *ex nihilo* has now taken on the general form of wealth generator, thus investing in work organisations in which the human factor continues to be key will never be able to meet the expectations of the modern-day credit market. Postfordism has thus created the *final separation* between credit and enterprise, and a paradoxical situation is now emerging in which the extreme form of economic liberalism represented by self-employment is being entirely sucked into the sphere of state aid, with regard to financial support for its fixed capital investments: subsidised loans, non-repayable contributions, tax incentives, and so on. An interesting example of this is the experience of Law 44 for southern Italy, which provides "start-up capital" for self-employment initiatives. But how can such activity be conceived when an industrial policy is totally lacking? And how can such a system sustain itself unless it is based on a system of assistance and information, enabling the self-employed worker to be guided in his choices? There would at least have to be an agency capable of *dissuading* people from embarking on a business activity that does not offer good prospects or at least putting them in touch with micro-enterprises from the sector in which they would like to work, in order to obtain the information needed to shape their actions. In this regard, the excessive importance attached to the network of personal acquaintances and above all to the *personal talents* of the aspiring self-employed worker brings about the risk not only of prolonging the *first phase* of the self-employment economy but also of taking a cultural step back towards the era of slavery, when a man was judged for his ability to work by examining the muscles of his arms and legs, the state of his teeth and degree of malnutrition.

Resources needed to stay in the market

Sociologists and economists studying the phenomenon of self-employment have focused in particular on the conditions that have enabled its birth, but not on conditions that enable such workers to remain in the market. The western world is obsessed today more by *job creation* than *job maintenance*. The chances of micro-enterprises remaining in the market appear to be quite slim, seeing their high mortality rate. There are no agencies or institutions that monitor the average life of an individual firm, a partnership or similar enterprises in the sectors of manufacturing or personal and business services. Thus we still do not know the reasons why a micro-enterprise fails or succeeds, except for the obvious ones (more work done, readiness to reduce rates). It appears that the liberal professions generally have a better chance of surviving, but this is probably due to their special status, only partly similar to that of second-generation self-employment, which we are looking at here.

It is thus a field that offers no analytical reference points.

It is said that product standardisation is rather poor in the sphere of self-employment. But is this a limit or a real resource of self-employment? Might not the constant need to enhance quality by seeking innovation be the biggest collective resource available to self-employment? And is standardisation not its death? The difference is seen clearly when looking at large and small consultancy firms. The former proposes as their strength the standardisation of procedures and products, while the latter are forced to seek innovation all the time. The former can be protected by a *copyright*, while the latter must subject their product and service to the expectations of the customer with each new job order. There is no doubt that semi-self-employed workers enjoy an advantage, since the

131

degree of prescription of their position is very high; thus the combination of work intensity and flexible remuneration appears to be essential to keeping them in the market. In both cases, however, in the work of the "true" independent worker and that of the para-subordinate worker, the *updating of knowledge* factor has a strong bearing, often related to the upgrading of technologies (e.g. the use of computers). Upgrading costs are extremely high and rise as the market grows, leaving the protected local setting and entering a national, European and global dimension. There may be some truth to the theory that the outsourcing by businesses or public administrations of functions requiring a high level of cognitive and specialist knowledge is a result of the strategy of outsourcing the costs of retraining the workforce in a rapidly changing world.

If that is so, one of the biggest demands that self-employed workers might make is undoubtedly that of having a share of the wealth of instruments in the public sphere for the updating of knowledge. The internet now offers access to a vast array of information that facilitates the updating of specialist knowledge. It is true, however, that much of the bibliographic material available in public institutions, such as universities, is not always accessible to the general public, especially the most valuable materials, namely the most recent publications, which are often difficult to access, even for students paying tuition fees. The demise of the Fordist corporation is also leading to the disappearance of the great corporation libraries, or sometimes these libraries become of purely historical value, an item of industrial archaeology, and are no longer viable as an instrument for the updating of knowledge. In this situation, knowledge is sometimes hidden away, and self-employed workers become Molière-like characters, jealously guarding their microscopic nuggets of knowledge. Tax incentives in place for reference material costs are in no way sufficient to reduce the costs of retraining for the turnover of the micro-enterprise. Conferences and study workshops organised by professional associations or ad hoc institutes have now reached a critical point between the cost of attending such initiatives and the quality of information provided.

In sectors in which texts, graphics and advertising are processed, usually in the media sector, where the levels of product standardisation and prescription of procedures are much higher, the incidence of *technological updating* costs can be a question of life or death for the micro-enterprise. The same goes for Postfordist crafts, for which investments in sophisticated equipment, required to stay on the market, are reaching levels that that are beyond the resources of the enterprise.

In short, if we look at the resources needed to enter the self-employment market and the levels of unemployment that make this an increasingly forced choice, we can see the need for such resources only growing in the future, and if we look at operating conditions and the resources needed to remain in the market we can only imagine a sector that has *reached its limits of growth,* and one that is destined to shrink rapidly. Bearing in mind that the majority of "human capital" is concentrated in this sector, that the incidence of fixed capital costs is growing constantly, and the fact that specific assistance is not provided by institutions or policies as regards the preservation of "human capital" and fixed capital investments, we have to conclude that Postfordism is preparing the way for the elimination of that middle class that was to have replaced the old working class.

Beyond certain limits, the intensification of "self-exploitation" cannot free up the economic constraints being imposed by the self-employment market, nor can it prevent the loss of those moral resources (self-realisation, job satisfaction) that had been the reason for the rise in productivity of self-employment compared with alienated salaried work, and thus for the great success of Postfordism. Policies aimed at dismantling the old welfare state are now conceived solely as "throwaway" policies, not as a means of rebalancing and redistributing the advantages and protections between subordinate employment and self-employment. The implicit social pact agreed to by self-employed workers with the Postfordist system (deregulation of work in exchange for currency value security) now stands on increasingly fragile foundations. Independent workers can play a part in furthering disinflation policies, i.e. protecting their liquid assets, as long as this carries a guarantee of their "middle class" social status. But when the accounts of a micro-enterprise no longer make this social recognition viable and when the disposable income of the self-employed worker goes below the bread line, such a pact is at serious risk.

The Market

This is a key difference between salaried work and self-employment status, between employee and self-employed. The resulting change in mindset is radical. Entry into the world of salaried work means leaving the market, taken to mean a condition in which one can continually redefine the boundaries of one's existence. The self-employed worker, on the other hand, is *permanently in the market*: he is employed until he delivers the latest job, can spend a long time without an income, and must continually put aside resources for the times no work is coming in. The notion of risk forms part of the mindset of self-employment; thus the service provided always contains some "promotional" aspects, with the self-employed worker seeking to continue relations with the client or to procure new relations. The fear of periods of inactivity means that the self-employed worker is a slave to market demand. One of the reasons for the intensification of work is that it is the practical impossibility of measuring supply on the basis of available resources; supply must have an almost unlimited degree of elasticity. An order that is refused is a customer lost. The anxiety of the "void" on the horizon often prevents the active self-employed worker from enjoying the fruits of his labour. One of the myths of self-employment is that of the freedom to take a break ("I can choose to have a holiday whenever I want"). The employee has an exact perception of any loss in earnings, the wage form of remuneration enabling him to monitor his economic situation. The self-employed worker, on the other hand, does not have such an exact perception; thus he is crushed between delivery deadlines and agreed rates, without being able to establish, barring some forms of non standard work, whether the volume of work needed to perform an identical job is more or less in relation to the unit of time. No matter how much money is put away, it cannot banish the anxiety regarding possible marginalisation from the market, and spending on consumption is often an implicit compromise as regards quality of life. As the micro-enterprise begins to become established in the market, planned leisure time, instead of growing, becomes less and less controllable. As an employee, the job routine acquired over time makes it possible to better schedule one's leisure time, while with self-employment the more experience one has the less it is possible to plan one's spare time. Becoming established in the market means more earnings and more commitments, almost never a limit placed on exertion. The employee goes through a period of insecurity during his apprenticeship and when starting work at the enterprise, but thereafter enters a period of serenity. In an initial phase, the self-employed worker goes through a phase of uncertainty, during which the effort to learn the unwritten rules of the market is to some extent fascinating and attractive.

The hardest phase is when the self-employed worker becomes established, realises he is caught in the market mechanism, and thinks he will never be able to get out of it. "You work more and more" is the comment most often heard.

In this regard, there is a big difference in mindset between the self-employment conceived by youngsters as occasional work and *consolidated* self-employment, performed by those for whom the profession is a social identity. As mentioned in the paragraph above, the biggest problems arise in the consolidation rather than the learning/start-up phase. It is then that the state of insecurity rises, and the sense of risk is felt most keenly. The state of the self-employed worker "in the middle of the journey of his life" is marked by the level of consumption attained and standard of living typical of the middle classes, completely removing him from a culture of scarcity and poverty. Reactionary attitudes may enter his mind unless he manages to construct a network of mutual help, unless he manages to forsake competitiveness at all costs and mistrust of colleagues, unless he manages to construct cultural and social areas of interest outside the working sphere. In a society that continues to be dominated by caste privileges and cliques such as those in place in Italy, where repetitiveness beats innovation and power takes on mafia-like connotations, where the public administration is perceived as a burden and not as a service, where markets are *captive* and professionalism is viewed as a moral attribute and not a saleable commodity, self-employment is still clinging on to the

1980s boom, but does not appear to be able to handle a serious market crisis or a mutation of the international division of labour. Younger generations appear to have forgotten about their rights. A strong return to subservient mentalities brings a return to the myth of dependent work assisted by public intervention. Among self-employed workers dependent work again becomes attractive, but we must have the courage to warn them that in the future, particularly where the protective barriers of national states will be torn down and the market will appear in all its harshness, the prospects of salaried employment may increase in terms of quantity but will deteriorate in terms of quality. It would be better if second-generation self-employment could find forms of alliances and self-protection.

Self-employment can but find forms of regulation, which will return it to the heart of a culture in which the notion of work was associated with at least a minimum guarantee of survival. The same holds true for temporary work. Forms of regulation of non standard employment will lead to the re-creation of collective workplaces, just as today there are forms of *intra muros* organisation of self-employment. But the most important collective place is one that is still to be conceived and built, where self-employed workers can *talk about their experiences* and be represented outside the sphere of the service they provide, a space wholly dedicated to sociality and alliances.

The organisation and representation of interests

The history of alliances forged by vulnerable subjects is closely entwined with the organisation of work; the same holds true for forms of conflict. Salaried work has passed through four basic phases of organisation and representation of interests: i) mutual benefit societies, ii) local trade union organisations, iii) industrial trade unionism, and iv) the institutionalisation of collective bargaining. This evolution has however been wrapped up in a system of cultures and ideologies promoted and organised by the workers' political party. Social democracy in Germany, the labour party in the UK, the Italian and French socialist parties, rejigging Marxism in the form of a *vulgate* easy to comprehend for the masses, at least in the period from their origins to the First World War, basically *shifted* the status of salaried work outlined by Karl Marx *to the social sphere*.

The actual status of salaried work was established with the affirmation of Taylorist work organisation and of Fordism, catching off-guard the parties of the Second International and their approach to the social question. Phenomena that would today be likened to the "globalisation" of the labour market, causing millions of emigrants from Europe to move to the Americas at the beginning of the century, caused the frontiers of national labour markets to be breached and throttled policies for solving the "social question" pursued by parties of the Second International and compliant forms of trade union representation and negotiation. Industrial unionism as a form of alliance of interests in the Fordist period is somewhat different from the "trade association", which represents a continuation of the old-style trade unions. The social question is defined starting from the factory, and not vice versa. The large factories, not the territory or nation, were now the space within which social relations, and workers' rights, were defined. The welfare state was not a modern version of the previous century's *Poor Laws*, rather it was a form of organisation and management of the deferred wage of the worker in possession of an open-ended contract. The salaried work status contains the citizen's code of fundamental rights.

The forms of conflict and negotiation change in the same way. The modern culture of salaried work cannot be conceived without the form of conflict that is called strike. Modern democracy in turn cannot be conceived without the freedom to strike. Modern dictatorships are marked by their suppression of three rights: the right to free political alliance, the right to a free press, and the freedom to strike.

Abstention from work, an action with which workers remind civil society and politicians of their essential function, can only by a collective action, a form of conflict that presupposes social cohesion, a community of intents. The more concentrated the workforce is in a single socio-technical space (large Fordist factory) the more effective this form of conflict can be. The evolution of the strike and of strike techniques is another interesting chapter that helps us to understand the evolution of the statute of salaried work. Bearing out the central political and legal role of the large factory, it was only with Taylorism and Fordism that industrial conflict, particularly in strategic sectors, took on the importance that the general strike had acquired in the period before World War I. In the Fordist era, the general strike ceased to be an instrument for re-negotiating social relations and became a defensive weapon, to counter coups d'état, for instance. In short, it departed from the sphere of an alliance of interests and became a political question. It may be a form of defending or re-negotiating deferred wage aspects, but it is increasingly a form of deputisation on the part of trade unions in relation to political parties.

The most important way that the explosive strength of the strike has been tamed is that of institutionalising trade union negotiations, from enterprise to state level. As Robert Castel describes well in his book on the metamorphosis of the social question, during the course of this involution, contractual bargaining becomes diluted and eventually loses its power to govern social relations.

This long digression was necessary to provide a clearer picture of the specific aspects of self-employment. Naturally, strikes are out of the question for self-employed workers, and this in itself defines its relevance as regards questions of representation. How can we imagine collective action if it is not possible to use the historical instrument of labour conflict? Scattered throughout the territory, self-employed workers do not appear to have a social-technical place where collective action can be organised. With no

141

collective counterparty to oppose and absolutely no possibility of retaliating directly against their clients, these workers have actually left behind the age-old history of labour conflicts and the system of rights that had been built upon recognition of the legitimacy of such conflicts. In other words, they have exited modern democracy and its operating mechanisms, primarily the mechanism that guaranteed the visibility and representation of vulnerable subjects. One of the key differences between the culture of salaried work and that of self-employment is the extent of juridification of social relations. Salaried work was able to protect contractual clauses entered into with the employer via the tools of conflict and negotiation, instruments accepted by civil society, whereas, should provisions be breached, the self-employed worker can get clients to comply with the contract only through the legal system. Our psycho-social structure is probably not fully aware of the enormous loss of space for action that civil society enjoyed before Postfordism or of the mutilation suffered by democracy. Other spaces have naturally opened up, and the path of democracy can take us towards unimagined horizons if more vulnerable groups are able to take such paths. Labour conflicts increasingly appear to be destabilising and subversive actions, particularly those that still have the potential to achieve the "normal" effects of a strike, i.e. to interrupt industrial production. With the creation of networked enterprises, decentralisation of production and outsourcing of services, conflicts that cut off links between the various nodes of the network cause a paralysis. Think of the devastating effect of strikes in the transport sector: in just a few days, they succeed in paralysing not only a country's production set-up but also the production/distribution cycle of global players. Postfordism too has its Achilles heel, but a democracy is not built on the negotiating power of a single category, rather on a type of power that can be wielded by all entitled parties.

Isolated from the historical form of conflict, and consequently from the historical form of labour representation (trade unions), the statute of self-employed workers may build alliances for itself and protect collective interests only through instruments that do not contemplate conflict, at least in its historically determined forms. Of the historical forms of alliance, only the mutual benefit instrument appears to fit the bill. So, from the point of view of an alliance of interests, self-employment appears to have returned, like a game of snakes and ladders, to the initial square. The concept underlying the mutual benefit society is that of supplying services to its members; therefore self-employment may gain sufficient self-protection only when it has devised all possible forms of service that can be provided in an effective manner. As we live in a "service economy", it should not be too difficult to plan and implement such a system. Trade associations and professional associations too base their legitimacy and representation on their ability to provide services.

With its being impossible to pursue conflict and negotiation as part of the employment relationship, the coalition of interests of self-employed workers vents its anger in protests against the State and, accordingly, the fiscal question is as relevant now as the "social question" was in the 19th century.

Citizenship

The sociologists of Weimar identified in the augmented nationalism of the middle classes, of which the self-employed sought to be a part, a replacement for the lack of class identity. Today we find ourselves in the presence of unsalaried work that has been expelled from the system of rights of salaried work (the right to a wage as a guarantee for subsistence, right to the welfare state, right to strike), and appears to have become estranged from the nation-state and from the state itself as an administrator of rights and collective resources. The sense of exclusion from such citizenship, as a consequence of the exclusion from the civilisation of salaried work, leads to a two-fold recognition of belonging: to the local community as a space for constructing networks of personal and family relationships and to the global community as a space for the virtual market. The self-employed worker fluctuates between these two extremes, the first hugely concrete and reassuring, the second feared and coveted at the same time, just like all spaces of the possible. They too can be the replacement for a national citizenship that no longer exists.

From the empirical data in our possession, we may state that only a tiny percentage of self-employed workers operate in the global market. It seems that only a few categories of *knowledge workers*, or "symbol analysts" as they are called, have the privilege of attracting a global client. Nothing compared to the millions of proletarians looking for a wage, who for decades have had to cross the world's oceans. Anyone thinking that globalisation should increase the mobility of self-employment, would be wrong. The mobility of workers over the territory of Italy is minimal, in a fully Postfordist era. The Postfordism of industrial districts has strong local roots; the self-employment of the new tertiary sector is concentrated in some metropolises (Milan, Rome); self-employed workers working for public administrations remain bound to the local seat of the client (which is almost always the residence of the work provider).

The problem of citizenship is not one of territory, it is a problem regarding rights: how to materially establish and exercise rights, a sense of belonging to the place and to the set of relations that are a source of income, but also the construction of a virtual/imaginary space where denied rights can be recognised.

Self-employed workers are accused of not having a sense of national solidarity. This charge is often levelled by groups or castes that enjoy social privileges, privileges they would not have if labour markets were truly global markets and if Europe were truly a space without legal borders and national regulations. These are generally social groups that have access to public resources. The nation, or the state, therefore represents the protected space for their privileges. Why did nobody complain to Italian emigrants about their lack of attachment to the homeland, even though they were leaving home to the sound of "Italia matrigna"? Why are self-employed workers only blamed for protesting against high taxes and not commended for the crucial contribution they make to flexibility and job levels? Think of the craft sector, for example. Were it not for self-employment, Italy would already be in an irreversible state of manufacturing decline, thanks to the very poor administration of public sector industry and the absence of innovation in part of the private sector. The financialisation of the economy would have continued without problems, and we would now be living in a society of raiders and raiders' boot-lickers. Were it not for self-employment, basic computer technologies would not have spread to all members of society or would have cost much more.

With the national reference to citizenship having been ruptured, self-employed workers have made a great contribution to civilisation, restoring the value of universalism and competence, and a "do-it-yourself" culture that was at the heart of the first mutual societies, with the birth of the culture of self-management of vulnerable persons. This culture was suffocated by Statism and by the welfarism taken up by parties of the workers' movement and by trade unions. On the plus side, the Statist culture has produced the welfare state, education and healthcare for all. However, in the 1980s and 1990s the system lost its flexibility due to a culture of mafia-like privileges, with some having access to public resources or an oligopoly of visibility in the media system.

Self-employment must not give up its conquests, which have often been the results of its very exclusion from the system of salaried workers' rights. It must not turn back towards citizenship cultures that are not in keeping with its material condition, such as the culture of the nation-state. Its social identity, its social recognition has been built around the relations between local and global, where it has its spaces of freedom and the possibility to make the most of its human capital.

But such an identity, located somewhere between two extreme poles, must not be the justification for a permanent "absence", an alienation from the concrete places of coexistence, places that are not networks but nodes of a network. Indeed, self-employment must put itself forward as a city administrator, as a *universitas* of competences, of cognitive resources acquired in its dual role of job and enterprise, as a builder of "places", and as a protector of pragmatism and innovation. In short, it must take its stateless status and go forward civic-mindedly.

Translation by Paul Warrington

FROM GENTLEMEN TO MERCENARIES
THE IDEOLOGY OF PROFESSIONALISM
AND ITS CRISIS

The volume that the International Labour Office has dedicated to the figure that most people associate with the successful professional — the management consultant — is a rather bulky one. Published in the mid-1970s and revised several times in subsequent decades, it is a collective work with the contributions of some authors who would go on to become *stars*, such as Roland Berger. At a certain point the question is posed: "is consulting a profession?" The answer given is very significant:

> We can call management consulting an emerging profession, a profession in the making, or an industry with significant professional characteristics and ambitions (…) but it may not be so important to decide whether consulting is a profession. Consulting has demonstrated that is can exist and prosper without any such decision (…) Even now, and even in sophisticated business cultures, virtually anyone can call himself or herself a management or business 'consultant', and offer services to business clients without any diploma, certificate, licence, credentials or registration.[1]

---

1   International Labour Office, *Management consulting. A Guide to the profession*, ed. by Milan Kubr, fourth edition (Geneva, 2002), p. 131.

This reasoning could be extended to all the cognitive activities that are performed by persons presenting themselves on the market as independent, or self-employed, workers, but not belonging to the categories defined as the "liberal professions" (physicians, lawyers, architects, etc.). For such persons, it may not be important to know whether their activity is entitled to be called a "profession", or whether they can put the word "professional" on their business card, as the ILO says. What is important to them is a favourable market situation, and the willingness of the client to pay well within an acceptable period of time. Unfortunately this is not what happens, since from the mid-19th century onwards the term "profession" has taken on symbolic meanings that more or less identify a social status. We should not throw this away without having thoroughly examined its history. An even bigger reason to stop and discuss this before moving on is the growing tendency of many associations of "new", unregulated professions to adopt alliance and representation processes similar to those of the liberal professions governed by "Orders". We believe that this is not the right way to go about things, as we can see from the history of the term "profession" and from the changes to the culture associated with this symbology in the various stages of modern industrial society.

Back to the origins of an ideology

There is no shortage of material for those seeking to examine more closely the mental construct that has been called the culture, or ideology, of professionalism. Literature on this subject is rich and varied. We have decided to begin with a text which, in the mid-1960s, opened up a season of very lively debates on the relationship between cultures and the formation of social classes. A text that took a rich historical view of the stimuli coming out of that restless but bubbling society of the time: *The Culture of Professionalism*, by Burton J. Bledstein.[2] The term *professionalism* contains the idea of "specialism", and this may be the best translation, since Bledstein's thoughts relate in particular to academic specialism, in other words the institutionalisation of knowledge in a jargon-like, largely rhetorical, form. This sets in motion self-referential behaviour and social constraints (the academic career), but also refers to the birth and development of *professional expertise* in general. This is something more than the single profession, a social role that is recognised and often exercised in the form of self-employment. Bledstein places the birth of professionalism in the second half of the 19th century, when America was attempting to set itself apart from the Old Continent, in any way

---

2   *The Culture of Professionalism. The Middle Class and the Development of Higher Education in America* (New York: W.W. Norton & Co., 1976).

it could, rejecting class distinction in society and constructing a national identity based on the idea of a single-class society — the *middle class* — in which neither aristocrats nor proletarians would exist. The ingenious solution to this problem was to put forward the meritocratic ideology as a criterion for explaining social differences. Such differences did not actually exist as the result of age-old divisions, handed down from generation to generation, nor were they a product of a political system designed to maintain them. They were simply the result of an individual's greater or lesser success based on his talent and ability to compete. This ideology could be channelled via the culture of professionalism, "a culture that worked wonderfully for individuals aspiring to think very well of themselves".[3] It was a powerful vehicle, as it worked not only on people's ambition but also on their insecurity ("perhaps no system of puritanical thinking has managed to use the insecurity of people as successfully as the culture of professionalism"[4]). The meritocratic ideology and the myth of the *self-made man* were of course an essential part of the "spirit of America" a long time before Bledstein wrote his book. His interpretation was however quite original, not so much for recognising the intrinsic value of that ideology, as for giving to the ideology a body, a clearly-identified social figure, that of the specialist, the *professional*. We may well ask then whether this

---

3   Ibid., p. 81.
4   Ibid., p. 101.

figure was a contradiction in a single-class society, since *professionals* inevitably form an *élite*, thus they end up being faithful more to the conventions of their language than to the truth. And they become more and more influential, since they are entrusted with the job of forming the ruling class, in particular university teachers. Bledstein however criticises not the esoteric language, but the "specialist" language, or the specialist mindset. His interest is aimed at high-level education, as the book's subtitle clearly reports, and only briefly addresses the problem of interest to us, that of the knowledge professions. But we know from the studies of brilliant Americanists[5] that at the time he is talking about, the late 19th and early 20th centuries, the large American corporations had discovered the benefits of employing independent or salaried knowledge professionals in order to enhance their external image (*public relations*) and to improve relations with staff (*human relations*). These initial experiences led to the management consulting market, which on the one hand led to the creation of large multinationals, having a size similar to that of their clients, but on the other to the creation of a parallel market of independent professionals who joined and added to the "business services" sector.[6] Three Austrian emigrants to the USA,

---

5   Fernando Fasce, *La democrazia degli affari: comunicazione aziendale e discorso pubblico negli Stati Uniti, 1900-1940* (Rome: Carocci, 2000).

6   Matthias Kipping, *The Consultancy Business in Historical and Comparative Perspective* (Oxford: Oxford University

forced to flee Nazism, paved the way for "business consulting": Peter Drucker, in the area of management theory, Paul Lazarsfeld, in marketing, and Edward Bernays, Freud's nephew, in public relations. From the 1920s a market of knowledge workers (or *brain workers*) began to develop in Europe too, providing services to the media, advertising, mass culture and entertainment sectors, drafting texts, creating graphics and so on. They were mostly *freelance* workers, or supplemented their earnings in this way to bolster insufficient income earned from artistic or literary vocations. *Professional expertise* became a practice that was recognised by the Fordist production system and by the metropolitan environment. When Roosevelt's New Deal was announced, freeing up fresh resources, the role of "expert" was incorporated in the administrative machine, within government agencies. In some campaigns it took on a value similar to that of *social worker*, i.e. a person called upon to forge a link between the hidden or unspoken needs of society and the welfare state. At the same time, as more and more technical and scientific knowledge flowed into the world of corporations, and it became necessary to deal with the problem of obsolescence of techniques and skills, there began to develop a form of training provided from outside the public

---

Press, 1999); Matthias Kipping, Lars Engwall (ed.), *Management Consulting. Emergence and Dynamics of a Knowledge Industry* (Oxford: Oxford University Press, 2002).

educational system. This heralded the first appearance of a *freelance* market. It was immediately blocked by two factors: companies' predilection at the time for internalising skills (Fordism is the prototype salaried society); and the ever growing interference of the State in economic and social matters, which resulted in many self-employed professionals becoming civil servants. The *freelance* market would only grow again and then explode in the 1970s and 1980s, following outsourcing processes, and the gradual withdrawal of the State from the provision of services.

Italian restraints

In Italy, things went a little differently. Here we will not go through the history of the recognition of professions in this country, but it might be useful to mention two or three things offering thoughts for reflection on the question of non-regulated professions. In the early 20th century some professional organisations (e.g., the association representing family doctors of the time) had been founded, inspired by socialist and Mazzini-based ideologies. They had relations with the "Chambers of Labour" and with workers' trade unions. The worker movement as a whole was not however able to understand the changes going on in the middle classes, and it failed to appreciate — despite having an excellent view — the meaning of the emergence of *technical* professions further to the success of Taylorist and Fordist systems. These professions would go on to serve enterprises and public administrations, unlike traditional liberal professions that focused on providing personal services. The Fascist movement on the other hand immediately grasped the relevance of this change.[7] In 1920 the Italian Confederation of Intellectual Work was created in Milan, and the Trade Union of Intellectual Work was founded in Rome a year later. Laws establishing professional orders and colleges were being promulgated continuously between 1923 (architects, engineers) and 1939 (labour consultants), but there remained for a time, in the corporative system, the signs of an original "trade union" set-up, of a claims-and-bargaining attitude, that took a long time to get away from, especially in a "new" profession such as that of engineering, practised chiefly within enterprises (1,530 engineers

---

7   Marco Soresina, *Professioni e liberi professionisti in Italia dall'Unità alla Repubblica*, "Quaderni di Storia", May 2003. Literature on the history of professions in Italy is dedicated almost exclusively to regulated professions. Here we have considered aspects of a historical and methodological nature holding good for all questions of professionalism, as well as an analysis of *technical* professions (pp. 165–201 of the book), as their evolution is closely related to that of the enterprise, and the "new" unregulated professions generally belong to the business services sector. A more thorough analysis has been undertaken more recently by Maria Malatesta, in *Professionisti e gentiluomini. Storia delle professioni nell'Europa contemporanea* (Turin: Einaudi, 2006). Chapter four is dedicated to engineers: 'Ingegneri ed élite', pp. 199–244. Refer to the bibliography herein for further references.

were entered in the Register of Engineers in Milan in 1935, while 1,346 were trade union members). The Fascist regime wanted to completely replace the liberal model of professional independence recognised by the State with the corporative model, which treated the intellectual professions in the same way as other work sectors, thus denying them special status. In actual fact, a compromise was reached: when it was in their political interests to extol Italian discoveries regarding synthetic products, fascism recognised the profession of chemist. The Republican government acted in the same way in 1962 when, in light of the success of the National Hydrocarbon Agency (ENI, Ente Nazionale Idrocarburi) in the sphere of power and energy exploration and supplies, it recognised the profession of geologist. In terms of recognition, there has been a close relationship between technical professions and the development of innovation in manufacturing.

"The case of engineering clearly shows that the origins of professions other than the 'classic' professions (...) should be viewed in relation to the radical transformation of capitalism", writes one of the most important scholars of the phenomenon in Italy, "changes to the division of labour in the large private and public organisations continuously create new specialist jobs, many of which set out to gain a professional status".[8]

---

8   Willem Tousijn, 'Tra Stato e mercato: le libere professioni in Italia in una prospettiva storico-evolutiva', in *Le libere professioni in Italia*, ed. by W. Tousijn (Bologna: il Mulino, 1987), p. 28.

The National Association of Italian Engineers was founded in 1919. Four years later the Order of Engineers and Architects would be established, and higher education would be reformed, as a result of which those coming out of technical schools were denied access to University. In 1933 the State examination for admission to professions was instituted. This process was going on at a time of great unemployment. It was this shortage of work that led engineers to form a pressure group. Throughout the fascist period inter-professional conflict among engineers, architects, surveyors, industrial experts and land surveyors continued to bubble on the surface. It lessened only in part after the end of the war with the building boom of the 1960s.[9] Italian history also shows that the market, taken to mean a set of factors that transform production methods and consumption styles, was decisive in conditioning the rise and fall of intellectual professions. According to liberal doctrines, the market is a self-regulating system. As we know, however, it is a system that produces distortions and inequalities. Conflict within the technical professions remained high in the 1960s and 1970s. With the liberalisation of access to the University in 1969, industrial experts and surveyors could become architects and engineers. This led to a boom in courses offered. Controls on access

---

9   "Il problema della disoccupazione dei tecnici caratterizzò tutto il periodo tra le due guerre", Fabio Bugarini, 'Ingegneri, architetti, geometri. La lunga marcia delle professioni tecniche', in W. Tousijn (ed.), *Le libere professioni*, p. 323.

to the profession, one of the main tasks of the various professional Orders, became a purely formal act. Moreover, independent professionals, or freelancers, those who were self-employed, were pressurised by the competition of engineers and architects, employed by Public Administrations, who would put their name to projects on a *part-time* basis or as a second job, often performing undeclared work. The situation appeared to improve only when the new "Regions" market opened. But this only demonstrates once again that the claim of possessing an exclusive skill is strong when demand is weak, and weakens when there is work for more or less everyone. This is a self-defence system, and has nothing to do with ethical codes and exclusive knowledge. But since the professional services market is dominated by demand, these self-defence mechanisms do not serve to re-balance the situation. Their impotence is thus transferred to the internal dynamics of the Order itself. This creates power cliques and episodes of nepotism, the victims of which are younger Order members or members without friends in high places.

The liberal professions are in reality a set of occupations basically united by an *ideology*. This ideology has been successfully promoted by the élite who have power over some particularly prestigious occupations (in particular physicians and lawyers), and has spread in capitalist societies thanks to its similarities with the dominant ideology. It has also claimed victims among social scientists themselves.[10]

---

10   Willem Tousijn, pp. 14–15.

Whether or not you agree with Tousijn's theory, the past experience of professions that have been recognised publicly and are organised in Orders in Italy appears to back him up. Incapable of re-balancing the ups and downs of demand, they have created inequalities within the same profession. What is more, they have not succeeded in monitoring the quality of work performed. Can we say that the Order of Journalists has prevented the degradation of information and the style of the media in our country? Has it even tried? And if even the most protected profession of all, that of university teaching, has not managed to oversee the quality of lecturing staff, or to reject the claims of those not qualified to stand on the lectern, how can we hope that less protected professions might do better?

When in the early 1980s the "new" professions in business and personal services began to emerge, the Order model was already wearing thin for those professions that had been granted public recognition.

Today, just as in the past, the Italian Orders perform bureaucratic functions. They merely ensure that new members are compliant with the law, and have no power to govern access to the profession. The latter is governed by State examinations. There is no other way of explaining why professions that have their own Orders have seen such a big rise in the number of members in recent years[11]

11   Maria Malatesta, *Professionisti e gentiluomini. Storia delle professioni nell'Europa contemporanea* (Turin: Einaudi, 2006), p. 349.

Look at lawyers, for example: 230,000 in Italy, a figure rising by 15,000 each year. The Order's Register for the city of Milan, in April 2010, had 15,600 members in the ordinary list, 3,200 qualified to practise the profession and 1,500 practising members. In December 2016, there were 18,749. "35% of the category's income is generated by 15% of lawyers. There are clients who do not pay, large law firms dismissing their staff, fierce competition, costly welfare schemes, aggravated by the phenomenon of "phantom" lawyers registered with the Order but not paying into the Lawyers' pension fund".[12]

Yet the assortment of interests that has formed around the Orders still manages to defend their role. Although the European Union and the Competition Authority took the official line of identifying professions and enterprises, in the end

The European Union gave in to the pressure of protected professions, diluting the pure form of liberalism by which its previous programmes had been marked[13]

While recognising that the professions, now treated in the same way as enterprises, are "subjected to an irreversible change in their nature and their

12   Luigi Ferrarella, 'Milano ha 20 mila avvocati (la metà di tutta la Francia)', Il Corriere della sera, 16 September 2010.
13   Ibid., p. 349.

functions",[14] a researcher such as Malatesta still believes in the special nature of professional ethics, the source of the reputation granted to the professional figure due to the social nature of his work. She cites the case of doctors and lawyers, who often work under extreme conditions. We would object on this point that if a doctor, instead of making money in a well-established surgery in Paris, prefers to risk his skin in war zones with "Médecins sans frontières", it is a choice deriving from his general view of the world and of political and social relations, or from ideological or religious beliefs, rather than being faithful to an ethical code of the profession.

Professional Orders again became a social force capable of influencing the State in the period of centre-left governments in Italy as the 20th century drew to a close. They managed to stand firm against the government's plans to abolish them in the name of liberalisation, in line with European Union policy. This once again showed that in times of difficulty some elements of the middle class can mobilise themselves successfully. However, they are not able to act as a "third force" among the social representations of Confindustria and the three main trade unions, CGIL, CISL and UIL. For at least a decade, in Italy and overseas, the question of intellectual professions has been converging, as Prandstraller writes, "towards the more complex question regarding *knowledge workers*". Professionals are

---

14   Ibid., p. 353.

a fundamental but not exhaustive part of a new social class, made up of the various expressions of knowledge workers.[15]

The first researches on knowledge workers that adopted these evaluation criteria appeared in Italy in the mid-1990s.[16] Finally the professions were not being studied in terms of sociology and debate on the opinions of different schools, but there was a return to the actual observation of reality, an empirical study of knowledge work inside and outside companies. Studies on work in the dot.coms, which grew exponentially in the United States up until the 2002 crisis, in particular those conducted by Andrew Ross, helped to sweep away interest in the question of professionalism.[17] The knowledge workers that formed a multi-form social stratum in the 1980s are something else. In the same years the Freelancers Union was created, an organisation protecting and representing self-employed workers. Finally a veritable trade union, a

15   Gian Paolo Prandstraller, 'Professionisti e knowledge workers. Il caso italiano', *Economia e Lavoro*, 2 (2003), 23–30; see also edited by the same author *Le nuove professioni nel terziario. Ricerca sul professionalismo degli Anni 80* (Milan: Franco Angeli, 1994), 4th Edition.

16   Butera, Donati, Cesaria, *I lavoratori della conoscenza. Quadri, middle manager e alte professionalità tra professione e organizzazione* (Milan: Franco Angeli, 1997).

17   Andrew Ross, *No collar. The Humane Workplace and Its Hidden Costs* (New York: Basic Books, 2003). See also Sergio Bologna, *Ceti medi senza futuro?* (Rome: Derive&Approdi, 2007), pp. 108–136.

form of association that does not seek to be different from those which, historically, sought to defend and represent workers. But in Italy this simple idea did not catch on easily. Even those who believe the profession to be an intellectual construct, agreeing with Pierre Bourdieu, and not a sort of human type, continue to think in terms of Associations being similar to Orders, whose role, among other things, is cast into doubt by those practising regulated professions. This was seen recently during the debate in Parliament on the reform of the legal profession.[18]

The distress and reawakening of the middle classes

Journalist and essayist Barbara Ehrenreich, through her website www.unitedprofessionals.org, has become a protagonist of the self-defence movement of American *white collar* workers in recent years. Her efforts are focused on salaried workers, but she is also in tune with Unions representing self-employed professionals.[19] She certainly cannot be accused of

---

18   V. Piero Ichino, *Libere professioni in libertà vigilata* on www.lavoce.info, 26.10.2010, and readers' comments; see also the website www.pietroichino.it.

19   The homepage of the site states: "For some time American professionals are no longer enjoying job security or the middle-class status they won with university studies and with hard work. In the current economic situation we are losing our investments, our health insurance and even our homes. But we still have our skills, and we can use them

incoherence in relation to her previous activities: she has been studying the *middle class* ever since the 1970s. In 1977 she wrote a two-part essay, alongside husband John Ehrenreich, on "Radical America", presenting a theory on the formation of a social class she calls "professional-managerial". Towards the middle of the last century this group would become a quantitatively relevant percentage of the US working population.[20] Its formation went back to the start of the century, the so-called Progressive Era, when a series of new professional figures were created, having the role of ensuring the social order of the capitalist system through the rationalisation of production methods (Taylorism) and of *governance* systems. That period marked the creation of the modern idea of "expert". The university system came into line with the emerging needs of society and of the production system. Important private Foundations such as Rockefeller and Carnegie promoted the development of this class, which was completely different from the traditional

---

to struggle and build a decent protection network and a fair economy. Join United Professional to build a mutual aid system, to work in favour of a healthcare reform and adequate unemployment benefits, and to develop an economy that has respect for our skills instead of wasting them and thowing them into the bin".

20   John and Barbara Ehrenreich, 'The Professional-managerial Class', *Radical America*, 11, nos. 1 and 3 (1977). In previous years the two authors had been engaged in the organisation of the US healthcare system and creation of the various professional figures operating in it.

"*petit bourgeoisie*", in which the Ehrenreichs include the *self-employed*. Up until this point, the schema is that proposed by Richard Hofstadter in *The Age of Reform* (1955), a classic that proffered the commonly accepted interpretation of the birth of 20th century American society. The Ehrenreichs however introduce an original twist, highlighting the fact that in the 1920s this class of "officers" of monopolistic capital began to rebel, in the name of professional ethics. They made great use of their Associations, and claimed the right to run society — considered as a business and administrative system — in line with the principles of efficiency. It was a technocratic utopia bound to be defeated.[21] "The characteristic form of self-organisation of the professional-managerial class was the profession". What are the key requirements for a profession to be called profession, according to these authors? The first is the existence of a specialist body of knowledge, accessible only after extensive experience; the second is the existence of ethical standards, which include *commitment* to the public interest; the third is a sense of independence from outside interference when practising the profession (only those belonging to the profession can pass judgement on the worth of the work performed by the individual). Reconstructing the history of a social group means helping to give it an identity. It is a fact that the modern intellectual

---

21　On technocratic ideologies and utopias, see S. Bologna, 'I lavoratori della conoscenza fuori e dentro l'impresa', *Annali di storia dell'impresa*, 17 (2006).

worker, the typical *knowledge worker* of today, originated from the time of Fordism and Taylorism. It is not possible however that back then there was any awareness that this group formed a class, for the reason that our authors rightly identify: identity was based on the single profession, thus there was no aspiration to be represented as a uniform class. Indeed, professions sought to stand out, to be different, even though lifestyles and common sense were the same in all professions. Identity was based on differences. We may view in the same way the early phases of the formation of the working class, prior to the phase of *industrial unionism*, when identification was based on the *trade* to which the union referred, much in the same way as the old corporations.

Max Weber and precarious workers

But let us return to the interpretative schema proposed by Bledstein and to the development of a culture, or ideology, of professionalism, which would in subsequent decades give to many self-employed workers a social identity and a sense of belonging. Reading those pages, we are immediately reminded of a text that remains a cornerstone in the history of studies on the concept of profession: Max Weber's 1922 conference on *Wissenschaft als Beruf*.[22] Where is

22   http://www.textlog.de/weber_wissen_beruf.html, translations by Sergio Bologna.

his starting point? A comparison between the American university system and that in place in Europe, and in Germany in particular. Before summarising the most interesting points for the purposes of our examination of independent intellectual work, we should recall that the German term *Beruf* contains a set of meanings that cannot simply be translated by the term "profession", even though the current term for defining a liberal profession in German is *Freiberuf*. When Weber used the term *Beruf*, he was fully aware that he was using a word that means not only profession, but also "vocation". Thus, when analysing why someone decides to embark on a professional path, he believes he has to take into account a number of *moral* conditions, which if lacking make it difficult for the person to practise that profession. "Passion" first of all, commitment to an idea of "progress" ("being overtaken is not only everybody's lot, it is the purpose of our work: we cannot work without hoping that someone else comes along and takes our work further"), and innovation, the idea that your mind suddenly clears, and you are illuminated (*Eingebung*), the need to think up something new (*Einfall*). The latter point has not been sufficiently examined by current interpretations of this text, yet it is of fundamental importance, because it means, in short, that if a publication that wants to be scientific fails to provide new ideas, but simply proffers a new interpretation, at best, or a rehash, at worst, of what others have written, it would be better off staying silent. This means that if a management consultant, in recommending organisational choices

168

to the management of a company, merely recycles in an elegant and attractive presentation what he was told in an interview with the company's CEO, he would be better off looking for a new job. But the fact that the conditions needed to properly practise a profession are moral in nature, or attitudinal, rather than intellectual, they must be measured in a social setting in which, as Weber says, "science has entered a stage of specialisation that was hitherto unknown, and will stay like that in the future", and "definitive and valid professional work today is always specialist work". The question regarding *Beruf* in the Fordist age — Weber knew the writings of Lederer, and of other sociologists of the time, and of his brother Alfred, and was perfectly aware of the revolution going on in work organisation systems — grew more complicated due to the increasing "technicality" of intellectual products, and the increasing specialisation of academic output, under the influence of trends coming from overseas ("the Americanisation of German universities"). The shift was not painless, as it caused changes to career paths. The first part of his conference address was dedicated to the way in which a youngster enters the academic world, comparing the different working conditions of a German *Privatdozent* to those of an American *assistant*, the former a precarious proletaroid, the latter a salaried worker.[23] Weber then touches upon a point that was

---

23 In Germany the youngster "answers to the Institute's director just like a factory worker, because the Institute

169

an important question in Bledtsein's text: does the progressive "technicalization" of intellectual products, the ever growing demand for specialisation, create problems regarding access to knowledge on the part of the majority of possible users, triggering a group or caste logic that gradually causes the *savants* of today to speak incomprehensible languages, and to act as if they were the priests of ancient religions moving their lips to voice expressions so incomprehensible as to confer ever greater authority to the priestly caste? Perhaps it is inevitable, but this question shows that if these contradictions are to be overcome, the answer cannot merely be a change in ethical attitude regarding the willingness to communicate more intelligibly. The logic of specialism is so far bound up in the vocabulary that other languages are not possible.[24]

---

director is convinced, in good faith, that the Institute is "his stuff", and acts accordingly, thus the youngster often leads a precarious existence just like any 'proletaroid'", in *Wissenschaft als Beruf*; Weber is one of the first to use the term *prekär* — present in the German language since the beginning of the century — and it is interesting that it is used referring to youngsters that aspire to follow an academic career.

24 The danger of an "incomprehensible" science is not the subject of Weber's criticism. He is much more concerned by the possible underestimation of the "moral" characteristics of the profession due to the progressive spread of technicality; the final section of the text is dedicated to a condemnation of lecturers that use their authority to spread their political ideas (it was the period of the strong social unrest of the Weimar Republic).

So is the creation of castes inevitable? In the case of "intransigent" professions, it is possible, whereas for professions open to the free market the logic is different. Viennese scholar Peter Drucker had read Weber's writings and had a perfect knowledge of 1920s Austro-Marxist literature, before he emigrated to the United States and became the founder of management theories, the daily bread of many professionals who chose management consulting as a job. It would be wrong to think that Weber and the social thinkers of German tongue of the 1920s and 1930s were unaware of the role of *Beruf* in the free market, both because they played a historically relevant role in defining the characteristics of the "entrepreneurial spirit" (*Unternehmensgeist*) and because they viewed the moral persuasions and state of mind of the scientist as being no different from those of a salesman or the founder of an enterprise, as Weber expressly states in the cited text. A *businessman* must also have passion, be committed to progress and be inventive.[25]

25　"A merchant or a big industrialist without 'business imagination,' that is, without ideas or ideal intuitions, will for all his life remain a man who would better have remained a clerk or a technical official. He will never be truly creative in organization. Inspiration in the field of science by no means plays any greater role, as academic conceit fancies, than it does in the field of mastering problems of practical life by a modern entrepreneur", Max Weber, *Wissenschaft als Beruf (Science as a Vocation)*.

Business and profession

A philosophy of "profession" in the free market is a typical product of American thought, which retains some very characteristic connotations. The first of these is closely related to the meritocratic ideology, the concept of *personal career*. In American thought there can be no professional ethics without the idea of success involving fierce rivalry with other professionals. Here lies the radical separation from the morality of the profession within the academic institution or from that expressed by the rules of conduct of the traditional liberal professions: physicians, lawyers, architects, etc. The problem of building professional ethics differing from that of the liberal professions thus covers all of the recent history of knowledge work performed independently. Although hospitals and the legal profession are today organised in the same way as enterprises competing on the market, success, in the form of social prestige and income, and the willingness to compete, are never indicated as being indispensable when choosing the profession of physician or lawyer. The ethical basis for these professions remains the codes of conduct that have been in place for hundreds of years. At the same time, when it comes to defining parameters to identify a new profession, and outlining the mindset needed to practise it successfully, the liberal professions model is naturally presented as the one that is easiest to imitate or repeat.

Weber speaks out at exactly the right time: 1922 was the year in which the first issue of the "Harvard

Business Review" was published. One of the first issues to be debated by the journal was "whether business can be thought of as a profession". This question is not at all rhetorical for those organising a business school, an important event in the history of America's university system. Many were aware that such schools had a promising future, as can be seen from the first articles in the journal written by lecturers of the Business School. In September 1923 the opening address to mark the Academic Year given by President A. Lawrence Lovell was explicit: the school had been created to meet the impelling demand for *business management* to be considered as a distinct profession, for which a specific educational path, and a special university, were needed. The resulting article drafted by Lawrence, based on this address, was published with the unfortunate title *The Profession of Business*, an ambiguous expression that can mean everything (every business activity is a profession) or nothing. The sense of his address was however very clear: here we want to train managers, people destined to occupy *executive* chairs in complex organisations. It was a lucid justification for the existence of a special university for managers. It did not however help to explain what a profession is. It might also have raised the question: is a university really needed to train managers?

In the months after the 2008 crisis, these debates from the 1920s re-emerged in the pages of the "Harvard Business Review". America and the whole business community were still in shock at the bankruptcy of

173

Lehmann Brothers. The big question being asked by public opinion, with a somewhat puritan leaning, was: "how did we get to this point? Do high finance wheelers and dealers, earning millions, not have a code of ethics they must conform to? Is there not a professional code of conduct?" No, and no, a professor responded in the "Harvard Business Review", since management is not a profession. If it were, Business Schools would not be Universities, but professional schools.[26] The discussion that began then, and that has continued in a lively, even agitated way in the journal's blog, allows us to gain some sort of an understanding, at the end of the first decade of the third millennium, of what the "common sense" of the *élite* understands by the term profession. Let us list some of the positions that emerged in the debate: a profession means mastery/control of a well-defined knowledge base and set of skills, it entails a fiduciary obligation in relations with the end user of the service (the individual professional must have an influence on the client's decisions); a profession is when the professional is accountable, financially and legally, for the errors he makes; when one is able to give a definition and to exercise control over the use of the title. "An activity deserves to be

---

26 Richard Barker, 'The Big Idea: No, Business is Not a Profession', Harvard Business Review Magazine, July-August 2010. The argument is not very convincing, as the manager's speciality would be that of "integrating" different competences and organisational structures. This can only be learned through experience, not at school.

called a profession only if some ideals, for example that of giving impartial advice, not causing damage, or pursuing the greater good, are infused in the behaviour of the persons employed in this activity", writes Joel Podolny, former chancellor of the Yale School of Management. "To be called a profession, an activity must have a code of ethics or a code of conduct", says another, and "a manager does not have it, and rightly so"; "the word *professional* may have had meaning a hundred years ago" — writes another — "but today the professional is like a craftsman, who learns a very technical, specific knowledge base in order to produce repeatable results, the profession is an organic set of skills that makes it easier to define standards", and again "these are discussions between university professors, who do you think is interested in the title, status, certification, code of ethics? Today people look at the results, and that's all!" It is indeed really difficult to understand the sense behind campaigns seeking ethical codes currently supported by Associations of professionals not protected by Orders. Already among the traditional liberal professions the code of ethics has become purely symbolic (has the German Order of Physicians expelled all its members involved in the social hygiene and race extermination practices of the Nazis?). What sense does it make to introduce a code of conduct for a professional when companies are allowed to systematically act illegally? In the era of globalisation is there a single concept of legality all over the world? Is it not the existence of different criteria regarding legality that determines the mobility of capital? Is not the search for impunity one of the great driving forces behind relocations? What should an ethical code produce: a self-regulating market? Those who have looked at the question from a historical perspective teach us that the ethical codes of professions have been an instrument through which a part of the middle class has attempted to regain social recognition in a period in which it felt crushed by the increasingly important role played by the anonymous face of large corporations in society.[27] It was a period when the professions were made to feel obsolescent following the acceleration of processes of innovation and the sizeable resources being invested by corporations in research. An early case of obsolescence of a profession was that of engineers in the early 20th century. Seventy years later computer experts would suffer the same fate. Now the phenomenon has become more widespread.

The rapid expansion of professional ethics after World War One may be wholly attributed to questions

---

27   Andrew Abbott, 'Professional Ethics', *The American Journal of Sociology*, 88, 5 (March 1983), 855–885; "in the early years of the 20th century the members of all professions underwent a decline in status... the spread of professional and ethical codes was a way of claiming back a lost status" (...) "the cultural and social phenomenon of professionalism defended the middle class from the new world of capitalism, the corporations, bestowing honour, dignity and security on the individual regardless of salaried employment" (p. 865).

of status. It was not the complexity of new competences that had made ethical codes necessary[28]

Perhaps it is the same phenomenon being repeated today: the insistent requests from Associations of unregulated professions for recognition as Registers, their insistence on the need for ethical codes, is perhaps their way of responding to the demand crisis and the devaluation of competences by limiting the offer. But it is a false and faint-hearted response, as we shall see further on, after we have focused on other aspects of the status of self-employed knowledge workers in order to understand the attitude to his trade that might create fewer contradictions. So let us leave on one side the question of ethics and take up again the discourse on meritocratic ideology.

Freelancing

Competition is thus a necessary factor for success. At the time when these new professions were sprouting on the market, and the respective professionals did not have immediate social recognition, and often not even specific university training for the profession being practised, two paths were available for obtaining such recognition: that of the traditional liberal professions, and that of economic achievement, reputation, in short professional success. Going down the first path means

---

28   Ibid., p. 881.

entering a territory reserved for powerful corporations which, rightly, refuse to give up their specificity and their own key to social recognition. An unknown country doctor is still a doctor, who can command the same respect as that reserved for the director of a university clinic. A *freelancer* practising one of the new professions finds it difficult even to tell his son what sort of job he does, with no academic title to certify his expertise, and no State exam to grant him public authorisation to carry out his trade. How can he be socially recognisable? The American answer to this question was the most pragmatic possible, and perhaps the most realistic: by becoming rich and famous. The ethics of success was fine by freelance workers of the new professions, i.e. persons unable to demonstrate they possessed special skills certified by academic titles, not protected by entry barriers, at the complete mercy of the market. The ethics of success and the related Darwinian ideology is thus identified with professional ethics. It is not a general problem for all intellectual professions, but a specific problem for those professions practised independently. A specialist employee working for a company does not have similar problems of social recognisability. First of all, he is an employee, and this is in itself sufficient to give him a social definition. His expertise is certified by the company he works for, by virtue of the fact that he has been hired to do that job, giving him the possibility of increasing his knowledge base with field experience. His career path is well defined by company rules (in the period in which the new professions emerged, when the Fordist system was at its peak, career paths within companies followed very rigid mechanisms), his pay is guaranteed, regardless of actual work performance (in that historical period performance-based pay was already starting to appear, but for employees it did not have the importance that it had and would go on to have for factory workers), his career path is channelled inside an institution. The risk for the *freelance* worker is quite different, thus the ethics of success is also a sort of stimulant to make success appear commonplace, almost within everyone's reach. You just have to want it badly, to put your heart and soul into it. The ethics of success forms a single mental unit with the ethics of *competition*, the mirage of success is the instrument to make the idea that man is naturally competitive, not only in the business world but in everyday life too, convincing. The next step is the most difficult one. The success of the professional belonging to the category we have described above does not follow the same logic as the success of an artist, such as a writer, actor or musician. That type of professional offers a *service*. The service logic is quite different from that of free creation of the spirit. Success accordingly depends on another, on the client, who acquires the service as a good, and reasons, acts, judges in a different way from the phenomenon described as "audience approval". First of all, the relationship between the independent professional and his client is very personal. It also has a bearing on the economic fortunes (or misfortunes) of the client, including his career prospects. If the audience member

179

does not like an artist's performance, he regrets paying the cost of the ticket, and that is an end to it. If the professional provides the client with a service of little value or containing incorrect evaluations, the cost may be high for the client. Therefore the ethics of success, which is natural in the artist, must be constructed artificially for the professional providing services. Here the simple philosophy of competition is naturally not sufficient. The other key factor comes into play: specific technical competence, which in German is *Fachmann* and in English the *professional*. *Fachmann*, Weber says, is the opposite of *Dilettant*, *professional*, Drucker says, is the opposite of *amateur*. But how can it be defined when there are no training systems to certify it? Once again, the answer lies in the moral and attitudinal sphere. It is not the possession of technical expertise that makes the professional, it is not the system of specialist knowledge and mastery of its use that makes an independent intellectual worker successful, it is not the technique that makes him an expert, rather it is the ability to relate to the client, the attention paid to him, identification with the interests and success of the client. This is the true skill of the professional. He must never forget that his job is to provide services, he is at someone's service, but is not his employee. In his search for success, the professional must be competitive, and must not have any consideration for his rivals. In performing his job not only must he have consideration for others, he must identify with his client, immediately understanding his needs and guessing his unuttered needs. The true professional must be able to win the trust of his client. *Trustworthiness* is one of the key words of professional ethics.

We should pay special attention to this passage. Lying at the root of professional ethics of self-employed intellectual workers, at the time it was deemed necessary to draft a code of conduct, the key requirement was not cognitive-intellectual in nature, rather emotive-behavioural. The mastery of the technique was taken as read, the simple training path was not sufficient. Technique was a question of experience, the key requirement for practising the profession was another: the mindset, the constraint of accountability, implicit in the term *Beruf,* which in the language of American professionalism is called *commitment.*[29] New professionals were taught that the giving of emotive energy is the main action of the work performed, superior to the expending of physical or intellectual energies. The dedication to work and the moral constraint in favour of the beneficiary of the service assume a high degree of acceptance of one's social status, a brain and a soul that are completely willing to sacrifice themselves to a different use made of one's time. In some professions an "impartial" spirit

---

29 The authors of chapter IX of the Sociology Handbook published in 2010 highlight the importance of these concepts in Weber's theory of professions: Vs-Verlag. de: *Handbuch Arbeitssoziologie, 2010*, Teil C, Alma Demsky von der Hagen and G. Günther Voss, *Beruf und Profession*, pp. 751–803.

is required. This is not so in most new professions which, serving businesses, allow the business spirit to seep through, thus they require a lifestyle where the career, that which is generally called "the professional's success in the market", is the main impulse for one's existence. In the 1980s and 1990s we witnessed a mass acceptance of this sort of conduct. Self-employed or salaried professionals, persons engaged in the roles of the *new economy*, women in particular, with a mindset and consumer lifestyle of the *lower middle class*, have played this modern comedy as one great choir, they have devoted their life to work, filled their minds with work-related problems, even outside working hours, often they have tolerated a wretched life, sometimes they have sacrificed their personal relations, spouse, children, friends. Work has lost its meaning of "services performed on behalf of third parties", and simply become a personal commitment, a test of personal strength, a mirror of one's identity. Not even the most avid forefathers of capitalism, or its blindest followers, could have imagined such a victory. In the end, the crisis induced a crack, a strong polarisation between those who found a reason to intensify their commitment, and those who began to become more detached from their "career". But the certainties, the singlemindedness, had been collapsing from an earlier time. Perhaps it was because of the greater commitment of women to work that the sense of detachment matured more quickly in the perception of gender. This was expressed in women's literature and essays, becoming a concept of working life as the opposite of a linear pathway, as a permanent "transition"[30] from one professional status to another, or as a "double yes", to caring for personal relations, working on behalf of third parties, affective and family ties, and the effort to raise the quality of professional services.[31] Ending with twenty-five pages of bibliography, the Chapter on professions in the *Handbuch für Soziologie 2010* stresses the importance of feminist thought in the demolition of ideologies in the sphere of professionalism. All the medals hung onto the professional uniform ripped off, the most recent researches in the German-speaking world talk about *Arbeitskraftuntermehmer*, of an entrepreneur of one's own workforce. All references to the profession as the common activity of a social group, a collective, disappear. Only the individual remains, his workforce and the market. Opinions have now converged that the turning point was the crisis of the Fordist model.

Management consultants: scourge or resource?

The figure of the management consultant is an example of how the problems of reputation, relations with the academic world and the public image of self-employment are sometimes inextricably tied up. It

---

30 Annalisa Murgia, *Dalla precarietà lavorativa alla precarietà sociale*.
31 'Immagina che il lavoro', *Sottosopra*, October 2009, edited by Libreria delle Donne di Milano.

cannot be denied that this "new" profession was very different from the liberal professions, mainly because it did not have specific training paths or exclusive competences. While the origins of this professional figure can be traced back to the period between the two world wars, it was only after 1945 that it took on an important role and ever greater visibility.[32] Some studies indicate the start of its spread to Europe from the time of the Marshall Plan. Studies conducted on the French case take its history back further, with the activities of engineers from the *Grandes Ecoles*, who instead of entering the Public Administration became managers in private companies. It is an interesting case study, since the development of what has been called the *consulting industry* gave rise to the creation of multinational companies, yet at the same time created that particular type of capital called "symbolic capital", possessed by persons enjoying a special reputation. Management consulting is an activity performed at the two polar extremes: in big-name organisations, and by the individual.[33] Of all professional activities, it is the one that has gradually come to symbolise individual success. When we think of a management consultant we instinctively associate

---

32   Matthias Kipping, Lars Engwall (ed.), *Management Consulting*, op. cit.
33   Regarding the Italian case, see Cristina Crucini's thesis, *The Management Consultancy Business in Italy: Evolution, Structure and Operation*, pp. 326, presented at Reading University in October 2004. I thank Matthias Kipping for having made a copy of it.

the figure of a sort of "guru", a successful, overpaid man, the quintessential professional. Often the figure of consultant is the symbol of the new professions, and of self-employment. The symbolic capital held by the management consultant derives from two light sources: management, the users of the service, and the university world, both of which enjoy the utmost prestige in our society. Someone has suggested a "symbiotic" relationship between the academic world and management consulting. This is because i) the figure performing this role sometimes occupies both positions, and ii) there have often been utilitarian exchanges between the position of university lecturer and that of advisor to powerful CEOs of big corporations. The consultant procures sponsors for the University, and in turn the University guarantees him a position of prestige and solidity. Alternatively, a Business School lecturer may open a consulting firm of his own and act as intermediary between the University and the company, procuring an intellectual workforce of guaranteed "scientific" worth. In this case the manager may perhaps procure less costly advice than that of the multinationals, who have to meet operating costs. The figure of the management consultant does however have weaknesses. The results of his work are difficult to gauge, the content of consulting activities is difficult to standardise, it is even difficult to describe the job. It is equally difficult to ascertain whether an organisation really needs external consultants. In short, the cost of consultancy almost appears to be a *benefit* for the manager, even a personal whim. The assessment of the consultant's work and of relative effects is reserved for the manager that hires the consultant. The manager will never be willing to admit he has wasted the firm's money. In this case too the relationship may often be symbiotic in nature. In the 1990s the myth of management consulting gradually began to lose its gloss. Criticism grew, with some people calling the use of the management consultant purely *theatrical*, serving only to put on a show. Poor in contents, devoid of ideas, the only thing the consultant had going for him was an ability to make a powerpoint presentation. But even if the consultant's ideas were excellent, they would be met by the inertia of the organisation in putting these ideas into action. The scandals involving auditing companies in the early years of the new millennium further shook the reputation of the profession. In Italy the notoriety of the consultant has often been attributed to his relations with politics and the Public Administration. Indeed, the term is sometimes confused with that of *wheeler-dealer*. At the other end of the spectrum, there are those who consider the management consultant to be the custodian of the managerial culture. It is difficult to make a balanced judgement, due to the weight of the tradition of professionalism and the importance of symbolic capital within the sector. The new professions have gained nothing by being associated with the archetypical management consultant, who in the collective imagination is a successful man demanding and obtaining astronomical fees for *quack doctor* services. We must completely put aside a system of thought conditioned by the ideology of professionalism in order to form a correct picture of consultancy, which is often effective in helping with the strategic choices of a company or a public administration.

The cited Consultancy Handbook drafted in the mid-1970s by the International Labour Office of Geneva and revised several times since then goes through the various schools of thought that have worked to outline the profile of the management consultant. There is however a central idea that everyone agrees on: that between the consultant and his client, the manager, there must be an exchange of knowledge, an interaction, and that both parties "must not spare any efforts to ensure that their working relationship becomes a mutual learning experience". In other words, this means that the consultant is performing *relational* work. Thus his expertise is measured primarily in terms of *personality traits* and *attitudes*, and only secondarily *knowledge* and *skills*.[34] Although the Handbook considers the offer of consultancy services as an industry that must have complex organisational structures, and devotes only four pages to the figure of independent consultant, there is no doubt that the real capital of the major consulting firms is the individual capabilities of its human resources. No matter how standardised their procedures, success in the market depends on the talent of single persons. Their clients are rich: corporations and public administrations. Resources generated by

34   ILO, *Management consulting*, p. 801.

the *management consulting* industry are sizeable. The result of knowledge acquisition and research work is an unrivalled accumulation of intelligence. Every self-employed knowledge worker, whatever trade he plies, may find in his literature reflections, experiences and analyses from which there is always something to learn.

Identity surrogates

It may have been subjected to fierce criticism, but the ideology of professionalism did not go away. It went through periods of economic, social and political crisis, and came out on the other side, wearing the same worn and patched-up clothes. But today, in the post-industrial age, there is something else that might explain why it was still with us even in positive economic periods, such as in Italy in the 1980s and 1990s, when the new professions emerged. It is unusual that professionalism came back into fashion when the middle classes were breaking up and imploding faster and faster, and there was a reverse trend to that observed by Bledstein and others in *Mid-Victorian* America. Back then the culture of professionalism bound together the various components of the "single class", while in more recent decades it has developed in a context of growing disintegration and fragmentation, floating like a substance that refuses to melt in the "liquid society", as Zygmunt Bauman puts it. The main reason for this may lie in the loss of power for work to provide an identity. Many studies have been devoted to this phenomenon, which is something we can all observe in our daily lives. People continue to be defined through the work they do, but purely conventionally, almost as if they give themselves a label, while deep down they seek more solid, convincing connections to characterise their personality. So there are two levels, identity as the mask in a play that we all act in, and wear in our round of superficial daily relations, respecting certain conventions, and identity taken to mean the parts making up our uniqueness. These two levels are often confused in a crisis of identity. In the former type, we can act the part or use the credentials, in the latter we must really believe it. In modern-day society this type of identity is tending to weaken more and more. As a self-defence reaction, this causes either a multiplication of the masks or the wearing of a disguise. In Italian society, where industrial policy has led the clothing and fashion industry to occupy a position such that it now forms part of the national identity, the construction of personality through clothes and accessories has reached breaking point, and has reduced generations of youngsters to soulless, walking mannequins. Thus, not only work has lost its identifying power, due to its non-use as a social value, and because job insecurity has weakened it of its existential meanings, but also the formation of personality has been made increasingly difficult and complex. In a setting of constant competition, it is the career, rather than the job performed, that creates the identity in the workplace. Those who are blocked from pursuing a career path refuse a definition of themselves through work. Here the ideological power of professionalism is triggered. As we have seen, though it may have been

189

structured in accordance with institutionalised *curricula*, it retains a grip on the individual through its moralistic component, and through its reference to the symbolic order of exclusive competence. So those practising one of the "intellectual professions" not only wear the daily mask, they believe in it too. It should come as no surprise that the "new" professions have been infected by the ideology of professionalism, seeking a form of citizenship and recognition in order to move from the status of *outsider* to that of *insider*. The short way of doing this was that through the old ideology. Then they discovered that they still stood outside the door. But that is another story.

Here it might be useful to take up again the question of the increasingly difficult formation of personality and identity through work, as it includes aspects that are closely tied up with the problem of our alliance.

The present day uncertainty is a powerful *individualising* force. It divides instead of uniting (...) the idea of "common interests" grows ever more nebulous, and in the end incomprehensible. Fear, anxieties and grievances are made in such a way as to be suffered alone. They do not add up, do not cumulate into "common cause", have no "natural address". This deprives the solidarity stand of its past status as a rational tactic and suggests a life strategy quite different from the one which led to the establishment of the working class defensive and military organisations.[35]

---

35   Zygmunt Bauman, *La società individualizzata* (Bologna: il Mulino, 2002), pp. 35–36.

Bauman's resigned vision is not thoroughly convincing. Insecurity is not just a product of precarious employment relations. Here we have the usual paralysing legacy of the subordinate employment model, the historically "stable" model. Insecurity is a result of the difficult formation of personality, caused in turn by the growing invasion of models — the persona, behaviour, thought, expression — transmitted by the media to our perceptive system when we are children and then adolescents. Each image is a potential personality. Images or words often transmit impossible personality models. Contaminating factors pour into the learning chains, dross of all types, before education is able to apply protective filters. We speak of education here only because of its higher levels, since the relationship between the formation of specialist knowledge and intellectual professions is binding. Hyper-specialisation was being criticised even before Weber, but the problem, as we can see every day, is not that of specialist languages being difficult to understand for the layman, or the claims to status of the professional élites, or even the discrepancy between the courses offered by universities and the skills needed by the market. It is not the specialist university, which works more or less. It is the people who cannot speak or write in their own mother tongue. What Drucker called *allgemeine Bildung* is increasingly uncertain and fragile. Specialist competences can be produced, and these can take on the guise of professional identities, but we are less and less able to produce personality, the set of attitudes that make it possible to mentally order knowledge and passions, know-how and emotions, that enables the individual to control, filter and channel the flow of incoming information, but above all to move along paths that he himself has chosen. This is the condition — we might call it a talent — that the self-employed worker of the new professions needs, the ability to move in all terrains, to navigate on water and fly in the air, to move from one market niche to another, from one system of relations to another. He does not need a professional identity, he needs a *personality* that can give him self-belief, thus the ability to take risks. He can easily discard the ideology of professionalism (although he must know what this is). It is not a paradox to state that for a *freelance* knowledge worker the most important requirement is a mastery of his mother tongue, both spoken and written, as it means he has a general idea of time and space, i.e. he has introjected the basic tenets of history and geography. It means he can express himself clearly as well as ambiguously, he has an idea of social relations, of when you can be frank and upfront, and when it is better to be guarded. *Allgemeine Bildung* cannot simply be translated by the term "general culture", it means a knowledge of the "fundamentals", how to recognise the essential from the superfluous, in a mindset in which the references of time and data hierarchies are clear, and the languages of information sets are recognisable. Literature, history and geography: it seems like intellectual snobbery, but how is it possible to form a personality without knowing how to read a history book, without being able to recognise the dynamics and genesis of the condition you are living in? Having explained to you in a passive manner what you are or how the world you live in came to be is like accepting the possibility that your mother and father are assigned to you by an office. Only a strong personality can produce fragments of original ideas, and offer the market what is generally called "innovation". This field is the non-exclusive yet specific field of independent knowledge workers.

Personality and writing

But what does "writing in Italian" actually mean? The masters of this art have allowed us to enter their laboratories, and to observe from close-up the tools of the trade. The majority of these masters are naturally experts of the literary art, but the drafting of reflective or expository texts has never been much different for them in terms of the quality of writing. The obstacles and the problems are the same. The great mystery lies in the sources of expression. Asked about the relationship between dialect and language in writing, and if he believed that dialect was a disappearing means of expression, the renowned author and university professor in Reading, UK, Luigi Meneghello said:

> I believe it is true that if a language dies, then a culture dies. Yet the opposite is also true, that the craft and rural world has been killed by the developments of our society, our civilisation. Obviously, it would make no sense to keep a dialect alive outside the society that

spoke it, or fed it. It remains to be seen how long it takes
for a dialect to actually disappear completely. But we
can assume that before it disappears the dialect can
deeply influence the development of literary Italian. And
that through mechanisms that are not too different from
the 'transportations' I have shown you.[36]

Industrialisation and Fordism had brought about
the devaluation of a linguistic heritage that literary
Italian had too often ignored, even repressed.
Speaking back in 1986, Meneghello could not
have imagined that ten years later the "progress
of civilisation" would bring the risk of a second
extinction, that of languages *tout court*. Could Post-
Fordism and the use of distance communication
techniques bring about such a disappearance? The
modes of "instant writing", "instant replies", the
introduction of soundless stylemes and graphemes,
legible using a phonology-absent linguistics, the
"removal of misunderstanding", Gargani says, quoting
Baudelaire,[37] the threat of a communication reaching
extreme levels of connectivity and becoming mutism,
are all questions that have got philosophers talking
ever since the Internet took over. They are problems
that can be perceived best by those that work with the
web on a daily basis, and can see the dangers. They
are the reserve not of philosophers, but of knowledge

---

36   Luigi Meneghello, *Jura. Ricerche sulla natura delle
     forme scritte* (Milan: BUR, 2003), pp. 119–120
37   Interview reported on www.intranetmanagement.it,
     Giacomo Mason's website.

workers. Languages in general have been, among the various indicators of civilisation, those most exposed to the threat of repression and prohibition. How many times has a language been "rescued"! Today this threat has changed face, what kills languages and associated cultures is not the prohibition of speaking or writing them, it is the monopolistic power of an idiom. It is this very threat that heightens this invaluable legacy. Italian, history and geography are essential, as we were saying, not only to give solidity to human capital, but also to form a personality, character. We are not talking about commonplace theories, or a certain snobbery, here we are revisiting issues underpinning the ideology of professionalism, which we can find in the writings of its founding fathers, as Bledstein again sharply brings into focus. One of the core principles, as we have already mentioned, was commitment, an ethical impulse to foster the public good, perhaps considered as more important than specialist expertise. But soon, *character* became an even more essential quality, "the distinguishing feature, the sum of qualities that distinguish one individual from another", which could well be what we have termed personality. Bledstein rightly notes that this "character" was meant as a self-image, self-belief, the individual's mindset when dealing with all situations, but only within the confines of the career. You must have *character* within the framework of *career patterns*. The term *career* originally referred to a racing track, and since the origins of modern professionalism "character" alludes to "a competitive personality". *Character*, having a personality. Here our mind races to Richard Sennett's book, *The Corrosion of Character*. This title alluded to the deterioration of character caused by the state of perennial instability of the modern worker. We want to go further in our disquisition: the difficult formation of character is the result of something more complex than an uncertain working situation or professional uncertainty. We believe it has more to do with one's perception of the world and with one's adaptation to the external setting. Post-Fordist production methods and globalisation have gone to create a new human anthropology. The spread of information technologies and use of the personal computer have introduced new epistemological parameters. This has radically altered learning dynamics, including the shift from childhood to adulthood. The IT revolution has enabled the very young to master computer languages and techniques, giving them the potential to become *hackers,* and to create great difficulties for, or even paralyse, sophisticated military apparatus systems. And no one taught them how to do it, they learned on their own. The computer revolution is a turning point in history, because it has put an end to the age-old system of human civilisations, which entailed parallel paths of natural human growth and gradual progress in terms of learning. The school age was a precise stage in physiological growth. Child *hackers* are a symbol of this cultural shift. Without any real learning path, without a school, they can already burst onto the scene of the adult world. The more it becomes computerised, the more this world is accessible to those who have not yet completed (or do not need) a school curriculum. If it is true that the main adaptability to the outside world is a knowledge of computer languages, and that all the "general education" culture is obsolete, or simply of no use in permitting the survival of the individual, then the very notion of individual personality clearly takes on a new meaning. Perhaps that notion of personality that we outlined earlier also belongs to yesterday's world. Is corrosion, the deterioration of character caused by job instability, called thus because Sennett's views, like ours, are dated? Does he need to know about child *hackers*? Of course not, but such a child does not even need relations, his world is there, on the screen, and he recognises it not through a map, but through the language of symbols. Clinical cases of youngsters who no longer go out, but stay in their rooms all day in front of the computer ought to give us some idea that the days of the android are close at hand. But we cannot say that things will end up like this. Only a snobbish and silly attitude resigns itself to a state of "looming barbarism". All totalising systems tend to reduce mankind to a set of soulless bodies, with no personality, capitalism first of all, with bio-capitalism not far behind.[38] The problem lies in the refusal to yield, to give in. It is the eternal struggle of the individual's freedom. Herein lies the core of the question on our alliance. But freedom cannot be separated from knowledge. Accordingly, the statement that computer technologies have created a

---

38   Andrea Fumagalli, *Bioeconomia e Capitalismo Cognitivo* (Rome: Carocci, 2008); Christian Marazzi, *Il comunismo*

different epistemology means that it has modified the parameters of the cognitive process, partly freeing it of the dependence on teaching, of brainwashing, of a dependence on manipulators of information, paving the way for the partial autonomy of the individual, albeit in a state of permanent tension. Speaking the language of symbols has narrowed the gap between the word and its effects, the gesture and its repercussions. It has lowered the stature of authority, and removed the pedestal. In this sense, it has played a role in the de-professionalization of our society.

The 'new' non-professions

The "new" professions emerged and developed in the period in which this shift in civilisation began to happen. They do not follow a predetermined educational path, they do not possess knowledge corresponding to a given jurisdiction, they live through relations more than competences. Their authority is established more by the market than by credentials. They do not need the frills of professionalism, indeed they are a hindrance. Yet the generic term "new professions" also includes some of the old professions practised in a new way, or

---

del capitale. Biocapitalismo, finanziarizzazione dell'economia e appropriazioni del comune (Verona: Ombre Corte, 2010); Cristina Morini, *Per amore o per forza. Femminilizzazione del lavoro e biopolitiche del corpo* (Verona: Ombre Corte, 2010).

rather performed in market settings so different from the original contexts in which they first emerged that they can be considered as "new". The difference lies in the *social form of the practice*, not the specialisation in itself.

Some have said: they are not professions, and those practising them do not have the right to be called professionals. Someone who has also been a scathing witness of the decline of the medical profession in the United States speaks about them with unconcealed disdain:

> Specialists who are mere technicians (...) serve their patrons as *freelancers* or *hired guns* (to employ both ancient and modern terms for mercenaries); their loyalties lie only with those who pay them. They accept the choices of their patrons and serve them loyally as best they can. In light of their specialised knowledge, such *servants* may advise their patrons to qualify or modify their choices, but they do not claim the right to make choices *for* their patrons, to be independent of them, even to violate their wishes. That however is the kind of independence claimed by professionalism[39]

Someone may feel offended by being called a "mercenary". The term merely mirrors the elite mentality, the attitude of social exclusion, distinguishing features of the professionalist culture. All of the principal scholars of the phenomenon —

---

39   Eliot Freidson, *Professionalism. The Third logic* (London: Blackwell, 2000), p. 122; Ital. trans. *Professionalismo, la terza logica* (Bari: Dedalo, 2002).

Freidson, Abbott, Magali Larson et al — are agreed on this point. Those who chose a new profession and self-employment in the 1960s, not only in Italy, did so with another mindset, one of egalitarianism. The German *neue Selbständige* were strongly influenced by "alternative" cultures and practices, by a sense of anti-capitalism, by a desire to flee from the cities to live in the country. When a computer expert chooses a *freelance* career he may have done so after an experience as a *hacker*. As Manuel Castells, perhaps the most important theoretician of the information society, of the *network society*, informs us, the term *hacker* does not indicate a saboteur, it indicates someone who rejects the ownership system, who considers the sharing of knowledge and experience as the highest value, the ethical principle that the IT expert living off the fruits of his work must conform to. This is the exact opposite attitude to that of exclusive competence, typical of the elitist ideology of professionalism. The Internet came about because of this anarchic-libertarian attitude. Even the computer was invented by virtue of an opposite mentality to that of professionalism:

> The personal computer was a serendipitous invention of the computer counter-culture, and the best software development was based on open source, and so was produced outside the corporate world, in the universities and in freelance ventures[40]

---

40   Manuel Castells (ed.), *The Network Society, a Cross Cultural Perspective* (Northampton, Mass: Edward Elgar, 2004).

The ideology of professionalism is conservative. It does not stimulate innovation. The modern knowledge worker has broader, more open horizons than those of the profession. In a 1995 text Keith Macdonald declared succinctly: "knowledge is an opportunity to procure an income".[41] If we agree with him, there is no point debating whether or not the self-employed worker paying VAT is a professional, or is entitled to present these credentials. It is not important to decide whether we consider him a mercenary or a gentleman. Let us plant our feet back on the ground, and return to his social condition, that which already thirty years ago had been uncovered by those who had foreseen the shift in culture.[42] Ever since the late 1970s the trend revealed by Magali Sarfatti Larson had been evident: the "proletarisation" of graduates.[43] Returning to our modern-day point of view, it is not enough to say that the impoverishment of intellectual work has actually happened, as had been predicted thirty years ago. Many things have changed over this period, this impoverishment has happened for reasons that had not been anticipated. Consolidated mindsets have been blown away, and been replaced by others. A historical tendency is never linear, it zigzags along,

41   Keith Macdonald, *The Sociology of Professions* (London: Sage, 1995).
42   C. Derber (ed.), *Professionals as Workers. Mental Labour in Advanced Capitalism* (Boston: C.K. Hall, 1982).
43   Magali Sarfatti Larson, 'Proletarianization and Educated Labour', *Theory and Society*, 9, 1 (January 1980), 131–175.

manifesting at turns, adding to its complexity. If we reason now, thirty years after the first alarm bells sounded on the impoverishment of intellectual work, we should highlight how people attempted to forestall it, sometimes using measures of pure survival, or with an increasing ability to administer one's knowledge, a shift from purely individualistic forms of living to networks of relations, serving as both a protection and as an source of new services. The market for the self-employed worker is partly that which he himself manages to create, or invent. But if the "market" form is inseparable from social recognition, it also means that one of the reasons for the lack of *middle class* reaction to impoverishment may be due to the fact that an activity that affords a high reputation or visibility offsets, to an extent, the meagre pay or shockingly low professional fees. Perhaps this is the real trap for self-employed workers: being bound to the values of social recognition as much as the working class has been bound to the values of consumerism. It is thus necessary to deactivate a number of ideological traps if we want to embark on a path towards alliance.

Federico Chicchi, someone who has studied in depth the question of identity and work, is right when he writes:

> the spread of a work culture that makes of individual performance and of the ability to compete in emerging markets the core elements of elevated social recognition appears to play a relevant role. Work helps to ascribe high status when it is seen as a risky, creative and responsible

activity. The attitude that tends to respect and admire those who agree to undertake risky and institutionally unprotected career paths. It appears to be part of a more general "risk culture" typical of Post-Fordist economic contexts (...) the 'risk culture' is thus an individualistic, meritocratic culture, which ascribes social value to the actor that acts without planning his strategy in detail, that assaults the market and does not undergo its effects, that tackles with determination and independence the conditions of uncertainty and variability of the Post-Fordist society (...) risking, then, becomes the main criterion of social value of Post-Fordism. Risking means being inside, not risking means being inexorably outside".[44]

But like with Bauman or Sennett, this again is just one side of the coin. It is a vision that is in danger of remaining within the "market" form. The real risk is not that of tackling the market. It is that of "thinking differently", rejecting the current mentality, not imitating the practices of the market leader. The real risk is that of innovating, of building up a unique knowledge base. *Querdenker* is a great German word, meaning one who has original ideas, in other words a lateral thinker. Innovation may include being able to reduce the unforeseeability of the risky action. The risk of the knowledge worker who practises an independent

---

44   Federico Chicchi, *Lavoro flessibile e pluralizzazione degli ambiti di riconoscimento sociale*, in *Identità e appartenenza nella società della globalizzazione. Consumi, lavoro, territorio*, ed. by Di Nallo, Guidicini, La Rosa (Milan: Franco Angeli, 2004), pp. 118–119.

profession must always be a calculated risk. It cannot be a leap in the dark, a complete gamble, it must be a relative risk. You do not think "differently" to dissolve ties with the client, but to bind him to more favourable terms, you do not think "differently" to be in a worse condition, but to feel more in control of a working relationship, no matter how asymmetrical the balance of economic power may appear to be. To calculate a risk you need your own talent, but to defend oneself against a risk, only an alliance with one's peers will work.

Tacit knowledge

A few years ago, in an essay in the Journal of American Medical Association, two authors, Epstein and Hundert, provided a very convincing argument that professional competence can be defined more as tacit knowledge than explicit knowledge.[45] Referring to Michael Polany,[46] they wrote:

> tacit knowledge is something that we know but normally do not explain easily, including the informed

---

45 Ronald M. Epstein, Edward M. Hundert, 'Defining and Assessing Professional Competence', *Journal of American Medical Association*, 287, 2 (January 2002), 226–235.

46 M. Polany, *The Logic of Tacit Inference* in *Knowing and Being: Essays*, ed. by M. Grene (Chicago: University of Chicago Press, 1969), pp. 123–158.

use of heuristics (rules of thumb), intuition and pattern recognition

Competence is a mindset, they wrote, referring in particular to medical practice. But we can take this idea, that *competence is a habit*,[47] and apply it to all professions, in particular the "new" professions, which are partly devoid of certification originating from a course of studies or from a specific academic title, and devoid of entry rules. The phrase that is often repeated in such cases, that "competence is a question of experience", or that "you learn only by practising a trade", is too superficial a description of the complex formation of a professional and of the knowledge needed to allow him to ply his trade. The concept of "tacit knowledge" however goes a lot deeper, as it indicates the set of theoretical, emotive, experiential, technical, moral, attitudinal and relational elements that make it so difficult to formalise, reproduce and transmit a competence. This is the true "secret of the trade" in modern-day professional knowledge work. Tacit knowledge is a form of development of identity, of growth of the personality throughout one's working life, it is true *lifelong learning,* but assumes the presence of a particular mindset, in other words being ready to absorb elements of knowledge, with due curiosity and humility, in relation to things and persons. In the universe of knowledge workers there

---

47   The title of an address by David C. Leach in the same issue of the "Journal of American Medical Association".

are, unfortunately, more and more human types and mindsets that take the exact opposite attitude, those who believe knowledge and competence to be a one-directional process, who believe their learning process to be complete with the formal handing over of the academic title and qualification to practise their profession. At this point, they have a purely hierarchical relationship with others: the users of their services. They are people who talk to you without seeing you, even if you are standing right in front of them, loathsome individuals, even dangerous if they work as teachers or doctors. But they exist only in the area of knowledge work. In the sphere of manual work their presence would be unimaginable. Why are these people devoid of tacit knowledge? Because with their attitude knowledge must always be a tool shown to, and shaken before one's interlocutor, like a stick in front of a dog, to ensure the other person's submission. In short, a form of arrogance. This is why the arrogance of the *knowledge worker* always goes with ignorance: it is inherent to a mindset that rejects tacit knowledge. This is technically possible only with the careful and inquisitive observation of the other, and affectively possible only with a touch of adolescent freshness. The multiplication of human types marked by this mindset in the modern-day knowledge society is both the cause and the effect of the devaluation of competence. They prove through a negative example the axiom that "competence is a mindset". And just as tacit knowledge is something that we know but normally do not explain easily, so the phenomenon of the spread of human types and mindsets, in which arrogance, presumption and ignorance/incompetence go hand in hand, is difficult to describe with the language of the sociologist. There are no empirical researches, case studies of this phenomenon, which we encounter every day. Were we to query the Internet regarding literature on this topic, what key word would we put? Yet every reader of this book will have encountered similar human types, and perhaps may have note they are dangerously on the rise, contributing to the degradation of habits. Both the social reputation of cognitive work and market value of competences are on the line. There is also a degradation of the dignity of language and writing. It is Meneghello again that describes the style they employ:

> What was annoying was not the obscurity, but the false obscurity, the pretence of the difficult, refined, unusual, profound. I felt offended right down to my bones. I felt that writing such prose habitually and by way of a trade (as some used to do) was not a dishonest way of writing, rather a dishonest way of living (...) for the people I am speaking about, it seemed the rule was: the less you have to say, the more commonplace and trite the contents, the more you have to render the way you say it obscure, twisted, allusive and convoluted.[48]

While competence is a question of mindset, the value of the academic title or of other types of accreditation is going down. We return to the

---

48   Luigi Meneghello, pp. 103–104.

question already broached: professionalism and moral attitude are inseparable. It makes no sense to ask whether *commitment* or technical competence is more important. Competence itself is largely a relational question, a question of how we act in relations with others. It is also a question of thought form, the structure of perception, which cannot be taught using learning techniques. We might indeed define tacit knowledge as what cannot be formalised in educational precepts or pathways, thus it confers on the individual the characteristic of being "unique" and unreproducible, and on the professional the characteristic of being able to do a service that no one else can provide.

We always go back to the problem that bemused Weber, and that will continue to puzzle those who will study this topic in the future: does not the standardisation of procedures and contents in specific disciplines, needed to make a mass university work, go in the opposite direction? Is turning competence into a reproducible technique not a way of killing that progress towards "uniqueness", as mentioned above? Does not higher education today serve to form languages of professional communities that are separate yet extended horizontally all over the planet? In the financial community, where the same language is spoken everywhere, where problems are presented, and assessed, in the same way, is not uniformity a key requirement for the utmost professionalism? The more we reflect on these questions, the more we are persuaded that modern knowledge work lives in the midst of these opposing forces, in a *permanent tension between tacit knowledge and formalised procedures*. Yet there is no question that the former constitutes a "competitive edge" for the self-employed worker, while the latter are mandatory requirements for a profession practised within a corporation. Whichever way you look at it, you can always see substantial differences between salaried work and self-employment.

Authority and authoritativeness

With knowledge work however there is a problem on top of that regarding social recognition or reputation. It is a more subtle and intriguing problem, that of *authoritativeness*. Here, the key words of "success", "competition", "commitment" do not help us to correctly gauge the problem. We can say that authoritativeness differs from authority in that it is a social recognition obtained outside the usual power mechanisms. Authority is partly synonymous with power. Someone is authoritative when his thinking and the way he expresses his thoughts acquire respect and prestige in a community. Authoritativeness is the pure essence of an intellectual superiority. It never overpowers other opinions, but it illuminates collective problems, the implications of which cannot be fathomed by most of us. Due to its very nature, it is a service to the community, free of economic needs, lust for power, or ideological interests. Weber holds that science, as a way of teaching, is an ascending process, on three levels: technical knowledge, method of

209

thought, clarity. Authoritativeness always includes an element of revelation, of unveiling. It is recognition by the community as a whole that certain manifestations of thought are illuminating, and thus of benefit to the community, which reciprocates with respect for those who emit these flashes of light. An authoritative figure is one who helps others to better understand themselves and the world surrounding them. The greater the detachment with which he dispenses his wisdom, the greater the prestige and credibility he will attain. An authoritative figure is unlikely to have attained the prestige he enjoys through success and money. He is never associated with someone who competes on the market and fights to obtain his prestige. At the same time, authoritativeness is not identified with moral authority. It may refer for instance to technical knowledge, a specialisation, and thus to a profession. Women scholars have worked very well on the question of authoritativeness. The process through which attempts have been made to commoditise authoritativeness is something quite different. The ruling powers and authorities (*Obrigkeit*) have always sought to impose their own form of authoritativeness, hanging the halo of authoritativeness above their heads. Today we have notoriety, fame, visibility, they even try to make a television presenter authoritative. The social dynamics behind this sort of manipulation form part of the most common phenomena of a mass society. Thus it is important to restore to the term authoritativeness its sense of revelation, illumination, and to reserve the recognition of authoritativeness for complex thought processes, typical of intellectual work performed as a profession. You might even say that a good weather forecaster is "authoritative", but that is something quite different.

Why have we introduced the subject of authoritativeness? Because we believe there is a discrepancy in relation to the meritocratic philosophy. While meritocracy is being touted by everyone as a social rule that can restore morality and order where corruption and disorder now reign, we do not necessarily agree that a meritocratic society is the best of all possible worlds. For the simple reason that meritocracy assumes selection, and selection assumes competition. In short, a meritocratic society is one in which the word *competition* is written in capital letters at the entrance to every town and village, just like in dictatorships the dictator's words or portrait is displayed. The meritocratic society is a market society. After what has happened over the past decade, it is difficult to imagine the market being capable of self-regulating, thus a meritocratic society should be equipped with rules and detailed selection procedures to implement the rules. Yet rules imply regulators, if they are to be complied with. If meritocracy were to be a universal principle governing social microprocesses as well, a whole population of independent and salaried regulators would be needed. Obviously this is not a real likelihood. Thus the meritocratic society is merely a utopia, hoping for it to happen is like invoking the appearance of the Virgin Mary. Not just in modern-day Italy, but also in the United States, and in 1920s

Germany. Weber again, in the text we have quoted several times, asks the question: once the American assessment systems are introduced in our Universities, what will be the basic selection criteria? The answer is chance (Hasard).[49] These words are prophetic, if we see what is happening today in the workplace, where personnel policies are governed by the trivialisation of meritocratic principles, their reduction to ridiculous and arbitrary assessment systems, which claim to be able to precisely calculate the performance of the individual and automatically his remuneration in terms of salary and career recognition. Employees are having to undergo the fetishisation of the meritocratic society. The commodification of authoritativeness is going in the same direction. For this very reason we have to restore to this word the dignity it deserves. With authoritativeness now taking on the caricatural guise of the "guru" figure, we should be striving to build models of a much higher calibre. To young professionals of intellectual work reading this, we would recommend that you seek to attain a status of authoritativeness, rather than pursuing success and notoriety. But perhaps there is no need, the ethics of success has lost credibility nowadays. Today more heed is given to a survival guide. But back at the beginning, when the ethics of the *professional*, salaried or *freelance*, was formed, and in particular in the period before the Great Depression of 1929, as well as in the 1980s and 1990s, the image transmitted

---

49   *Wisssenschaft als Beruf*, op. cit.

of the market appeared to consider success as a goal within everybody's grasp.

Transit, move, leapfrog borders

The professional ethics we have talked about up until now relates in general to the self-employed intellectual worker. But there are many professions, and each one requires its own identifying code in order to form a *community* with which the individual professional can identify. There is no doubt that these processes go back to the times of the guilds and corporations of medieval times. But we often forget that of the two purposes that their charters were created for — namely preserving the secrets of the trade and erecting entry barriers — the first has completely vanished with today's intellectual professions, and the second has become very difficult to pursue, as there are no specific educational paths, and the "new professions" are continually creating new figures, stimulated by the constant innovation, specialisation and globalisation of markets. Setting up entry barriers today in a world in which (in theory) the mobility of intellectual work is totally unrestricted is ridiculous and inefficient. Can a corporation of Italian web designers prevent a Lithuanian web designer working remotely in our market from practising the profession? It seems unlikely. So what good is an Association representing professionals? It may do some *lobbying* with the public administration and the government to free up resources or introduce legislation to make the profession less onerous for its members, or to enable them to operate in a more favourable context. It may guarantee its members long-term vocational training, and may offer a definition of the profession itself. The time we are living in today, even for self-employed professionals, is no longer the age of trade unions, it is the time of *industrial unionism*. It is no longer the time for Associations representing advertising agents, consultants, translators, and so on, it is the time for transversal organisations, who deal with problems common to all self-employed knowledge workers.

Few have worked on the question of professions as much as the prolific professor Andrew J. Abbott. His 1988 book *The System of Professions. An Essay on the Division of Expert Labour* is a classic. We believe that it bears out many of the arguments that we have attempted to expound here, and is particularly valuable because, unlike the authors cited until now, he takes into consideration not only the liberal professions and the professions for which there is a specific educational path, but also the *galaxy* of new professions that emerged in the 1960s and 1970s. Abbott believes that the key requisite for a profession to be such is that of being able to establish its "jurisdiction", i.e. the specific scope of its competences. But unlike those who, before him, had already singled this out as a distinguishing criterion, and had concluded that the task of a body protecting the profession must be that of defending its professional perimeter, Abbott rightly stresses that the thing that distinguishes the current age from others is the continuous trespassing of professions into the areas of competence of other professions, the effect of innovative processes demanded by the market. The result being a "system of professions" i.e. a fabric within which there are continuous shifts, continuous adjustments of the various spheres of jurisdiction. The provisional nature of the borders of competence is not only not harmful, but is actually desirable: "interprofessional mobility" is a dynamic factor for progress. Abbott thus completely overturns the convictions of those who believe that the borders of the profession must be continually kept under surveillance and, for example, that systems must be built to monitor access. The world, as well as the market, changes and moves on. The professional must move likewise, he may exercise one profession and then pass on to another, or, as happens more frequently, he may start in one profession, a specialisation, that turns into a new profession by virtue of its new contents:

> the social structure of professions is never fixed (...) the nature of them is constantly subdividing under the various pressures of market demands, specialization, and interprofessional competition[50]

In short, the professions have undergone continuous internal changes. This gives the professional more opportunities to survive and be successful, to invent new services or a new way of providing them.

---

50   Ibid., p. 84.

Moreover, one of the most evident phenomena we are seeing is that of the accumulation of different professional competences in a single person. "You have to know many more things than those you needed to when you started working, twenty years ago". Isn't this a phrase we have heard *freelancers* say thousands of times? Abbott's "system of professions" is an interdependent system, the more elastic it is the more efficient it is. Those who want to make it a rigid system, on the other hand, are simply shortsighted. But even if we want to defend these rigidities, and if it is right that every profession should resolutely defend its jurisdiction, who can actually do that, i.e. by resorting to legal actions (as there is no other efficient method)? Only a profession that is organised under a single national Association, only a monopolistic situation can permit an effective defence of one's jurisdiction. This is not the case for professions not protected by Orders, who are (unfortunately) represented in an extremely fragmented way. The most interesting aspect of Abbott's reasoning is that he does not believe that this jurisdiction should be left to the mercy of market forces and to its thrusts and counterthrusts. Indeed, the stronger the profession (the more a professional is sure of himself) the greater its ability to control a jurisdiction that is assumed to have been dissolved. Again, the more alive he is (i.e. the more a professional is competitive) the more he manages to integrate the knowledge base marking his specialisation with additional knowledge taken from other professions. Another interesting point in Abbott's analysis is the use of the term *expert labour*, as it is much more accurate than the term that we often use: "professional knowledge work". This term restores the sense of a generalised and specific condition of human activity, and does not allude to a social status. When we say the words "doctor", "lawyer", "architect", we are unconsciously led to think of a social status, not only a professional specialisation. Over the decades it has become generally established that these professions, and other more traditional professions, are synonymous with the term *middle class*. "*Expertise* work" on the other hand sounds like work that can be performed by many. It is anyone's guess if that is useful in attaining or maintaining a middle class status.

A *social status always hanging in the balance*

And here we come to an important point in our story: the relationship between professional work and social status. This is where we must totally revise the thoughts of Bledstein and of the Ehrenreichs, at least the 1977 version (while saving Barbara Ehrenreich's 2010 observations). These authors, as well as the whole of 20th century sociological literature, consider *professionals* — both self-employed and salaried — to be the backbone of the middle class, its "hard core". The underlying theme of sociological research has been the "constitution" of different strata of the population into classes. Today, the main theme is the "dissolution" of the classes, especially the class that shaped the Western lifestyle, the *middle class*. We have had an avalanche of studies on the "class" concept and on its not being applicable to modern-day society, which is marked by uniform lifestyles among social groups having very different incomes, on the fragmentation of society into groups and subgroups, on the complexity of the present day, on the over-simplification of theories that break society down into classes, and finally on the fact that Marxism is dead. Naturally, these theories also claim that the working class is dead too (it had to have existed in order to die, right?). Faced with these analyses, leading us through the mazes of social microprocesses, which are of course interesting, but in the end prevent us from seeing where we actually stand, we believe that the dissolution of a status that forms the essence of the Western way of life is a *macroprocess,* one that should rightfully be studied by sociologists and other observers of society. Perhaps not everyone is quite aware of the great significance of this macro-phenomenon. One of the best vantage points to assess its relevance is that of the professions, in particular the traditional liberal professions. *Expert labour* provided by a freelance worker working in the new professions is exposed to market risks, as we know, thus it cannot guarantee in advance the attainment, preservation or loss of a given social status. The liberal profession, practised independently, either because it is handed down from father to son or because it is held to be a protected market, is viewed as an activity that is subject to few ups and downs. This is no longer the case, however, partly due to the reasons given by Abbott. He uses the term "division of *expertise* labour", attributing to the term division the same meaning with which it is used in Marxist literature, namely a distribution of tasks constituting a hierarchical structure (*"an upper, truly professional group and a lower, subordinate one"*).[51] This argument should not be snubbed out of hand, since the most commonly accepted idea is that the basic reason for the lack of employment opportunities in the liberal professions, and thus the decline in fortunes of many young doctors, lawyers and architects, faced by job uncertainty and even poverty, is solely that of surplus supply. The solution to this problem would once again be to limit access to these professions, imposing limits on university enrolment. Yet in many countries we already have this, and it is not sufficient to rebalance supply and demand trends, due to the different rules on quotas in place in countries that go to form a single market (e.g. Germany and Austria). The reasons behind a "downgrading" process — a term commonly used in temporary employment agencies — must thus be different, and more complex. A few years ago a programme on German television showed young German doctors filling airport lounges on a Friday afternoon, waiting for Ryanair flights that would take them to Britain for the weekend to do an exhausting number of hours' work. They were doing this just to make ends meet. There are those who can see the funny side, such as the blog www.studioillegale.com, describing the daily vicissitudes of a young lawyer

---

51   Abbott, p. 128.

in Milan in 2010, doing all he can just to survive. The research Specula Lombardia told us that among architecture graduates, those holding a three-year degree are faring better, as at least they can work as furniture representatives, whereas with a specialist degree they would be considered *overeducated*.[52] The division of *expertise* labour between a stratum of professionals earning an income that allows a middle class standard of living and a proletarised stratum working partly for the former, on commission, is a structural fact, inherent to the logic of the profession. What has changed today is the period elapsing between a subordination condition, the *lower group* that Abbott talks about, and a condition that enables the professional to belong to the *upper group*. This period has grown so long that it has caused many to change profession in the meantime or to give up the profession for which they are academically qualified. While the crisis and implosion of the middle class are a fact, and do not need "statistical proof" to be accepted, the consequences of this crisis are unclear, with particular regard to the question of common sense. The term *middle class* has been used to connote lifestyles and mindsets that are common to social groups that previously had extremely different income levels. Therefore, when looking at the crisis of the *middle class,* the deterioration of economic conditions of given activities, something that is statistically demonstrable, may be considered as being

---

52   Specula Lombardia, *Il lavoro dei laureati in tempo di crisi*, June 2010, pp. 165.

secondary to factors of a cultural and attitudinal nature, which tend to create lifestyles that are hard to reconcile with actual income levels.[53]

As Ferruccio Gambino reminded us in an essay written twenty years ago, they have been talking about a crisis of the middle class in America since the 1930s. Over that time, the definition of *middle class* as a sociological category has been changing, due to the changes in the internal composition and social role of that section of the population and in evaluation criteria. The initial definition of "owner class" gave way to an identification with the role performed within salaried labour (white collar workers), with an evaluation criterion based on status changing to one based on income. While the word crisis has been bandied about so frequently, it does not simply mean that the *middle class* follows employment cycles like any other group of the working population, rather that each crisis has its own peculiarities. Each crisis affects a social group that has been given the same name, but is profoundly different within.[54]

The "imploding" middle class we are talking about is not that of post-World War II or of the 1930s, it is that of the *debt economy,* as Marco Revelli says, whose underlying morality is dominated by consumption levels.

---

53 V. Marco Revelli, *Poveri, noi* (Turin: Einaudi, 2010).
54 Ferruccio Gambino, 'La classe media come categoria della normalità nella sociologia statunitense', in *Tensioni e tendenze nell'America di Reagan*, ed. by E. Pace (Padua: Cedam, 1989), pp. 63–87.

The common denominator is the style of consumption, not income. The *middle class* is made up of those who want to be in that class, not those who are actually in it. In America the *middle class* that is today crumbling away is that created via credit cards, not secure employment. This has led to a veritable revolution in the accumulation model of capitalism, since the financing of the economy has been based on the impetus of individual indebtedness. Profits obtained through productive labour and investments in capital and knowledge have become a secondary source of accumulation compared with income obtained by borrowing money at a low rate of interest and buying high-yield securities. There is a stack of statistical evidence about the impoverishment or stagnation of employee income, much less on self-employment income. What little we have tells us that incomes have remained steady or grown for an ever-smaller percentage of the total, suggesting that for self-employment too the "central" band of persons has narrowed, and the hourglass shape has taken on a similar form to that of employment incomes in general. To examine more closely the implosion of the *middle class,* the experiences of real people count more than mere statistics.

Translation by Paul Warrington

ACTA, THE FREELANCERS' ASSOCIATION
Manifesto of Second Generation Self-employed Workers

Part One: About our work

We are a particular category of self-employed workers. We are not traders or farmers; we do not belong to those professions protected by Orders. Among self-employed workers, we are the most "modern", children of a system that has been called "Post-Fordist". We work in the universe, or market, of intangible assets. This is the market that has seen the greatest changes over the past thirty years in terms of business, society, technologies, organisations, education and human relations. We are required to possess complex knowledge subject to continuous change. This is not limited to specialist knowledge but also requires relational capabilities that cannot be acquired via specific educational paths. Those of us with the most professional experience began working in the late-1970s when there was a widespread desire to "go it alone", to challenge the market with all its risks, to reject the working hours and rules of the corporations. Our younger representatives were inspired by the promise of freedom arising from the spread of new technologies. They believed in an open society of knowledge workers without any entry barriers. Workers able to use the Internet as a new, liberating frontier, and able to do their job without any real geographic constraints.

We started out with a great desire for freedom and independence, confident that our professional abilities, competences, and human capital were sufficient to obtain social recognition and a healthy portfolio of orders from a number of clients. We are not willing to give up this idea of freedom and independence even though times have changed and the market has become a more difficult place. Neither do we want to give up the idea that it is great to work by relying only on one's own competences, spirit of initiative, ability to forge relations and communicate without having a fortune to back one up, without belonging to lobbies/pressure groups and the like, without having to bow down to others — in short, independent, serving first ourselves and then others.

1.1. For the past few years, and especially since the most recent financial crisis (October 2008), it has become increasingly difficult to practise our professions. For those that started 20-30 years ago, it is impossible to pull out, but for many of those who have just started this kind of work, the market risks are almost unsustainable. For some people, "obliged" to register a VAT number, the very word "market" appears to be a mirage. But we would not be who we are, namely persons willing to risk their own skin, trusting in one's own spirit of initiative, if we were to get bogged down by this situation, and go around moaning and grumbling. Our human capital, our competences, which we have so far invested completely or mainly in relations with clients, must today be invested in defending ourselves against the crisis, which has so clearly revealed (to those who had not noticed before) our extremely weak and disadvantaged social position as citizens.

1.2. Unfortunately, many people had not realised what was happening. They were convinced that having a trusting relationship with the client was enough to be and feel safe, that it was enough to work well in order to earn social recognition. Many convinced themselves they were an "enterprise" and thus enjoyed the prestige accruing to the head of the enterprise, as per the public image from the 1980s on. Some might even have proudly thought of themselves as "entrepreneurs", no longer being confused with humble "workers".

Many thought that risking their own skin and being "self-made" means being overly individualistic, rejecting any thoughts of sharing experiences and knowledge, convinced that colleagues, the ones who do the same job, are the main rivals.

Now we have to put our feet firmly on the ground and reject these illusions and beliefs once and for all.

So we are workers. Like it or not, we belong to the world of work, even though public institutions have not recognised us as such for a long time. We have not even been given a space in statistical tables. First we were placed in the (micro)enterprise group and then among "atypical" or "non-standard" workers.

Then we became lost in the confused galaxy of self-employment, among street vendors, farmers, physicians, lawyers and so on.

We are a special category of self-employed workers, not only the most "modern", the most topical, but also that with the highest growth trend. Unlike all other categories of self-employment, this trend has not stopped even during the crisis years.

We are the future of self-employment, of cognitive work. The market of professional work will be more and more dependent on us. But an awareness of the role our category plays leads to a parallel rise, among many of us, in disappointment in and indignation about the way in which we are considered and treated, both individually as citizens and collectively as a professional category. The impetus to organise ourselves and create networks also arises from the realisation of the large gap between a social and economic role for second-generation self-employed workers that is destined to grow and the continuing "denial" of their very existence on the part of public institutions. But things are changing, and they will change more quickly if we are organised and united.

1.3. Let us take a step backwards and offer a better idea of our condition. Let us return to the situation at the beginning. For many of us, the first stimulus to work as a freelancer was the desire for freedom and independence. The key requirement for being able to do so was a mastery of knowledge, know-how and professional competences, acquired partly through complex and varied educational experiences, partly through experiences in companies as employees, both accompanied, in many cases, by periods spent abroad. The "primitive accumulation" of human capital, taken to mean professional competence, a key requirement for the start-up of an activity, was an individual process for everyone, a particular experience. What is the main problem we had to face thereafter? The need to keep the value of that human capital, and even to see it grow.

But here our situation deviates considerably from that of other knowledge workers (for example, university lecturers and some categories of professionals that have super-protected their relationship with clients who do not expect explicit growth in individual knowledge). Our authoritativeness must be continuously "re-certified" by the market; therefore our knowledge must be continuously updated, requiring considerable emotional and economic investment. However, the system of "lifelong learning" offered to us by public institutions is increasingly unsatisfactory. This obliges us to take individual paths that often prove to be unworkable for reasons of logistics and cost. One reason that justifies the urgent need for greater cohesion and greater collective organisation of our category is that related to training, or rather self-training. In this field, we must procure the resources by taking them from the current system, which is inefficient and corporative, built more to support ailing organisations and bureaucracies than to offer a service. At the same time, a greater ability to get one's voice heard can give us the chance to help with the modernisation of higher education, so that it is less distant from market needs. We must take up this "historical" task, namely that of "preventing the devaluation of human capital in the age of the knowledge economy". This is not rhetoric, it is a matter of survival.

1.4. Our position in respect of the market is quite different from that of other categories of self-employed workers and completely different from that of salaried employment since we do not have to just meet a market demand. We must and sometimes are forced to "construct the market" or "invent tomorrow", which forms, in fact, part of our code of conduct. In other words, we have to cover the hidden, unconscious, implicit needs of clients. As there is often a turnover of clients, our activity is not only a non-routine one, but it has to be an innovation-led activity. In a world that tends to imitate and standardise values, narrow the taste spectrum, and reduce all actions to a standardised procedure, our desire/need for innovation may appear to be a "pie in the sky" endeavour. If we consider innovation not only in terms of technological upgrading or implementation of a product or process but also as a dynamic of social relations or construction of associative systems, we can see that the need for innovation is not a subject that regards just the relationship with the market but also mutual relations among all of us. The construction of a class or category identity, of "social systems", permits collective action and the sharing of identifying languages, in other words preparatory actions for the "representation of interests". This is just one of the many functions of an associative system. It is no coincidence that the most successful and authoritative organisation in this sphere, the Freelancers of the United States, was established thanks to the initial contribution of a Swiss Foundation that promotes innovation in social relation systems.

1.5. Ours is a way of working that depends considerably on the opportunities afforded by the Web. We belong to the Web generation. IT specialists alone are one of the largest groups in the category of freelance knowledge workers. For the first time in the history of human geography, the Web has created a virtual system of communication. This now appears to have taken over from the real-life system. It has created a system for accessing information that is becoming the primary source of knowledge, both trivial and sophisticated. The Web (and the tool needed to access it, the computer) has allowed us to work from home. It has made a crucial contribution to the domestication of work and has muddled the time spent working and time spent "living". It has allowed us to work anywhere we want: on the train, on a park bench, on the tube, in an airport lounge. It has helped to raise individual productivity and very often lengthened the working day well beyond the eight hours fixed by employees' employment contracts. The web has enormously lowered the cost of self-training, making us independent in our learning choices, with access to online courses tailored to our needs. The web has allowed us to promote ourselves, publicly offering our services in a global market. It has also given us the chance to work overseas without having to emigrate. In short, we would not be able to go on without the Web and would not be able to work. Indeed, the communication industry is offering us increasingly sophisticated tools for accessing the Web via mobile devices. There is, however, a difference between knowing how to use the Internet on a daily basis and being able to exploit all the relative opportunities in order to uncover all its secrets. The value of a freelancer's human capital now depends to a great extent on the degree of sophistication of his or her knowledge on how to use the Web and integrated communication systems.

1.6. Constant contact with the World Wide Web places us in a situation that presents some contradictions. On one hand, allowing us to work alone increases the individual's isolation in the long run; on the other hand, it is a very convenient way of communicating with our peers, thus enabling us to stave off our isolation. The Web is increasingly becoming the most effective channel for creating collective movements and mobilising forces. This may result in political events or wide-reaching forms of association. Creating a website or a blog has become the first action performed by those wanting to involve other people in a given initiative.

In the same way, the impetus to search for forms of alliance among self-employed professionals can make use, now and even more so in the future, of the opportunities afforded by the Web and of systems created to share knowledge and individual creativity using open source — thus economical — technologies. As the user base grows and interactive systems multiply in number, there is, however, a risk of the Web becoming an out-of-control Babel. The crisis of some social networks is to an extent a harbinger. Freelance workers cannot afford to be indifferent to the fate of the Web, if only because it is perhaps the only setting in which they can build and share their own thoughts as self-employed workers. They must, therefore, keep watch over any attempts to restrict access with the excuse of "moral control". We know very well that there is no moral regulator but only monopolistic and oligarchic powers that can intervene in this way. We can better exercise such control, to ensure that the cognitive democracy of the web is not restricted, if we are organised, united and identifiable. In this way, even those having a limited knowledge of the computer world can benefit from the experience of those experts. Together, we can create our own territory, our own social network, and get in touch with self-employed knowledge workers from other countries.

1.7. Working alone, communicating via the Internet, entails the risk of considering remote or virtual relations to be the only form of social relation. It is thus necessary to offset this tendency by making an effort to develop proximity relations, such as physical relations among people that look each other in the eyes, listen to one another, and rediscover the joy of conviviality. Proximity relations are important for lobbying actions and for collective events, including protests. It is not enough to "post" an opinion on a forum or send a signature via the Internet. You must show your face, and demonstrate that you are there in numbers if you want to be heard. Rediscovering the vocabulary and grammar of direct speech, thereby compensating for the abbreviations and shortcuts we use via email or text messages, as well as rediscovering the communicability and flexibility of spoken language in a certain sense means helping to preserve our civilisation as European citizens. We are the heirs of those who have, over the centuries, constructed the cultural, artistic, legal, technological and entrepreneurial values that are the foundations for our modern-day professional competences. Therefore, the revaluation of proximity relations should also be seen as a way of preserving and adding value to our human capital.

1.8. Apart from professional competence, the most important requirement for performing freelance activity is relational skills, the art of forging relations with what we call in a broad sense the "market". Here, there are no schools or guidebooks to steer the individual toward finding the best and most effective approach. What counts is the character and sensitivity of the individual, and above all experience. The ability to build relations is not discerned only when searching for and finding clients. It is also discerned when forging and developing a trusting relationship with the client, when agreeing on a contract offering decent terms, when finding one's way through the mazes of corporate hierarchies and bureaucracies without treading on anyone's toes, when building a long-term relationship with the client, when defending authorship of a project, when managing relations with collaborators, when receiving payments within reasonable time frames, and so on. These are things that require intuition, tact, initiative, astuteness, respect for others and, above all, respect for oneself. There are no schools or universities that teach these things, yet at least one general rule of conduct should be clear to all self-employed workers of the cognitive professions, in the collective interest of the category: to turn down shamefully low fees, not to agree to "dumping", not to give in to downward competition. In times of crisis, it is difficult to ask for consistency and personal sacrifice from others. And when one is working for oneself, there is no monitoring of the community. It is a waste of time pretending that the regulation of fees of professionals organised in Orders will make a difference. By working together, side by side, factory workers could control the "scabs" and put them under pressure not to fracture class solidarity. Here, too, we self-employed workers are alone, far from the gaze of others, and therefore more vulnerable. For this reason, we have to stick rigidly to this rule: "always refuse a job that pays too little". It is a rule that depends on the honesty of the individual and cannot be substituted by any State law or regulation.

Part Two: About our being citizens

Integration in the world of employment has taken on an increasingly pivotal role in defining people's relationship with the State. You are citizens as you are workers, enjoying benefits in terms of social and welfare protection, depending on the role played in the workplace. If you have a job, you obtain a residence permit. Articles 1 and 4 of the Italian Constitution are explicit in this regard.[1] This form of citizenship has been developing in the 20th century as a result of the spread of the industrial system and the big changes in industry, ways of thinking, and social structures, including, importantly, the birth and development of the worker/ trade union movements. If citizens have no real rights, there is no real citizenship. In the 19th century, rights used to be defined within the sphere of bourgeois values of freedom (political and religious opinions, the press, right to movement, etc.). More recently, values ascribe primary importance to social protection. This has led to the formation of a State that mirrors the "European social

---

1   Art. 1 "Italy is a democratic Republic, founded on labour", Art. 4 "Every citizen has the duty, according to personal potential and individual choice, to perform an activity or a function that contributes to the material or spiritual progress of society".

model", which is based on the legal form of salaried employment. Not even the fascist regimes dared to cast doubt on such a model. They considered civil liberties to be less essential for the purposes of preserving the State model, but in some cases social protection measures were actually intensified. The right to work, and legal systems based on contractual relations generally, substantially define the status of citizenship, also with regard to the sphere of freedoms. But things began to change in the 1970s. This concept of the State and of citizenship entered a crisis with the end of the economic model it originated from, a model basically founded on the mass production of goods for mass consumption and of capital goods. A "Post-Fordist" economic model came to be formed, focusing on the production of intangible assets: image, symbols, knowledge, communication, information, entertainment, leisure, taste, sport, finance and energy production. The "big factory", especially in countries such as Italy, broke up into a galaxy of small and medium-sized enterprises, in particular microenterprises.

The State is tending to withdraw from the production of goods and from the direct provision of services. The whole legal thought underpinning the "European social model" also entered a crisis, as did its conception of citizenship and its vision of the rights and duties of the individual towards the State and the community. The first to feel the adverse effects were those not included in its basic parameters, those not "contemplated" by that model — the "typical" social figure of long-term employee. Those to suffer first were we self-employed knowledge workers not represented by professional Orders, and the new generations of "atypical" workers.

In Italy, professional work performed independently by second-generation self-employed workers is not yet incorporated into labour law. Its legal status is defined by the Civil Code, in article 2222: "When a person agrees to carry out work or services for remuneration, mainly by means of his own labour and without a relationship of subordination in relation to the client". Our work consists of providing a "service", so our employment relationship ceases when the service has been completed and recommences when another service is asked of us.

The feature of "intermittence" is thus inherent in an activity such as ours, which is largely practised on the basis of orders with a limited budget. For some time, it has been said that we are sellers of services, free merchants of knowledge, mini-enterprises, and not workers, in relation with whom the State has protection obligations similar to those of employees in both the public and private sectors.

2.1. So we are recognised as citizens, but not yet as worker-citizens. What does this mean? Well, that we are recognised the rights belonging to the sphere of 19th century bourgeois liberties but not to the Fordist social security systems of the 20th century. Yet it is evident, in the definition given in the Civil Code, that our services are always provided in favour of "third parties". Thus, the fruits of our work are always enjoyed by others, and our work is recompensed with a remuneration. But that does not appear sufficient to create a legal entity of equal dignity to that of the employee. For this reason, to allow us to be incorporated into labour law, and the area of social protection, jurists increasingly believe it is necessary to add to the definition of self-employed worker the specifier, "economically dependent". The alternative is to move self-employment under the umbrella of commercial law, transforming what is an employment relationship into a purchase/sale agreement between equally ranked enterprises.

2.2. In actual fact, our relationship as citizens with the State is much more complex and contradictory. Once again we should take a step backwards and return to the "Post-Fordist turning point". What was the great change that took place in Western political and legal thinking that cast doubt on the Fordist social model? The answer: the idea that the State should no longer have the onus of social protection, allowing this job to be taken over by private services, indeed encouraging the move to a new system. What is more, the State should also transfer essential public services to private concerns, such as water and energy distribution, local and national transport, and telecommunication. In short, a shift of the entire public utilities sector to the private, with prices partly subsidised, and education, albeit more carefully, and finally the national insurance system, to be reorganised around a "second pillar", that of private pensions (supplementary pensions and so on). At the heart of this change there is a deal with citizens, which replaced the old Rousseau pact: the

State will reduce the services it offers but also the fiscal burden on citizens, or it at least promises to reduce it. Beginning in English-speaking countries, this change has conquered the European Union, and has become a frame of reference for the new concept of citizenship. The European Union is accelerating the process of so-called "reforms". In short, these entail: 1) a gradual withdrawal of the State from the provision of some services, 2) the removal of the burden of responsibility from the State in the sphere of social security, 3) an increase in job flexibility, which slowly eats away at the very concept of labour law. Looking at the results of elections in recent years, it appears that European citizens, who are mostly employees, approve of this change. We, born and raised in this mess, we self-employed knowledge workers, not recognised as one of the "intellectual professions" as per art. 2229 of the Civil Code, have been tossed around by these changes. And frankly we have not given two hoots about it. We have remained passive, unrepresented, without a "voice". In a world of corporations and lobbies, our lack of civic engagement as a category has yielded what it deserved: exclusion from decision-making processes, indifference, absence from the public space. Others have spoken out in our name, others have drawn up our profile. We continue not to see ourselves in their definitions. Can we go on like this? No — when the world changes, we have to change the way we act, too, or the least we can do is critically evaluate our attitude.

2.3. We began to raise our heads again when we realised that the deal replacing the Rousseau pact was not in our best interests. It was founded on a (short-sighted) exchange: fewer services, less protection from the public sector, fewer taxes contributed by the private sector. As far as the effect on us was concerned, the terms of the exchange were overturned: no protection, more taxes. Indeed, the first initiatives in which self-employed workers recognised themselves as a category were tax protests (the glue keeping freelancers together in the United States is welfare and social security problems, whereas in the United Kingdom, where they prefer to be called independent contractors, the main problem is fiscal in nature). We have said it many times, but it bears repeating: our situation, that of providing services to companies and public administrations with every interest in documenting costs in their books — and we represent a cost — and fulfilling their duty by doing so, is one in which it is not possible, materially or technically, to evade taxes. Our resistance to higher taxes, especially when there is no parallel rise in payment for services rendered, is not hugely different from that of the employee whose pay packet is cut. Curiously, the protests of the employee are deemed to be legitimate, even considered heroic in some cultural-political circles. Our protests, on the other hand, are treated as being incompatible with the responsibility that should be shown by citizens. Yet the tax burden on incomes, which in many cases are no more than subsistence incomes, is not just one of the problems facing the freelance worker, it is *the* problem. The charge levelled against us — namely that of reducing the question of citizenship to a matter of paying taxes, of practising particularistic selfishness, which has for too long become a cliché rolled out by sociologists and opinion makers, in particular those working as irremovable civil servants — does not take into consideration the fact that when the State divests itself of the obligation of guaranteeing the citizen's social security, the only tie linking the individual to the institutions is that of taxation. It is the only time when the citizen is in contact with something called the "State". We self-employed workers certainly cannot be accused of having eroded the values of the "public good"; rather it has been due to the greed of some financial and industrial institutions that have imposed market rules founded on the reduction of labour costs, or continuous pressure exerted by corporate hierarchies, in short a morality founded on collaborative ties under conditions established by only one of the partners: a relationship that is not contractual in nature, but disciplinary. We were not the ones to impoverish the concept of "public good"; this was done by a style of politics and governance concerned with safeguarding specific or even personal interests, a style that ignores the collective good. So if European citizens have fallen out of love with the State and passively accept it as being a privilege for the few, some responsibility must lie within the public sector, there must have been a "caste" attitude within some areas of the public sector. There must

240

have been some form of debarment and harassment of the individual on the part of the State bureaucracy.

2.4. The most evident and dramatic aspect of changing historical conditions, which have brought the idea of social security into line with that of citizenship in general, has once again occurred in civil society, in daily work relations. There has been a reverse journey from the path taken in the early 20th century, which led to the creation of the socialist and trade union movement, to "Christian social" thinking, gradually to the signing and recognition of the normative value of collective labour agreements and labour protection legislation, and finally the creation of the institutional framework called the "European social model". This backward-moving path did not begin "from above", i.e. by erasing from State constitutions some of the pillars of that model since, at least until 1989, there was either no political will to do so or insufficient parliamentary support, and the bureaucratic and corporative structures instituted through the model had created positions that were resistant to all types of change and largely indifferent to the interests of those the model sought to represent or protect. Italy's backward journey began in the mid-1970s, "from the bottom up", with the reorganisation of the enterprise, its fragmentation into many independent work units, often turning employees into "subcontractors", and bringing the maximum number of workers below a certain threshold that entitled firms to receive a certain level of protection. When the political and cultural climate changed with the collapse of the Berlin Wall, when the values of socialism lost their gloss, and when socialist and former communist parties became hyper-liberalist in order to save their seats in Parliament and their salaries, when Christian social thinking gave way to the integralism of the confession box, when new ecologist movements shifted policies away from social security and towards the environment, and when the privatisation drive got under way, especially in Italy (1992–1993), there was nobody left who was willing to defend the welfare state model that had been built in the postwar period. In the meantime, the bureaucratic and cooperative systems that had helped to create such a model, systems perceived by citizens to be a cost more than a service, were hard at work defending their positions. Within single enterprises, this reverse journey was like travelling on a train with no brakes: the management style and relations with employees changed in the name of flexibility, which is now in danger of becoming purely disciplinary, even limiting some basic civil liberties (one extreme example is that of labour contracts contemplating the dismissal of employees who pass on information about the pay they receive). The army of temporary workers and "atypical" workers created by this change in style and values within companies, magnified and partly justified by globalisation, has helped to raise the level of mistrust in a social model that runs the risk of resembling more and more an empty shell. The resulting loss of a "sense of State", the feeling of having lost an institutional and moral connection (one symptom of which is the high number of non-voters at elections) make the situation ever more uncertain and lacking in points of reference as regards citizens' rights. Legislators appear to be chasing after a reality that is changing too quickly, unable to prevent laws drafted with great effort from coming into effect too late, sometimes creating more problems than those they were meant to solve. Demand is growing for a suspension of new laws, especially in the sphere of labour, and a return to local bargaining, with social policy or labour policy measures aimed at specific social groups in particularly hard times, of a specific rather than general nature. In terms of the evolution of law, this transformation of reality appears to have brought an end to the "general rule". Fundamental principles such as "social equity", "respect for the individual's rights at work", and "opportunities for all", which are found in abundance in European Union documents, are now perceived as bothersome preaching unless accompanied by specific measures to be implemented quickly and easily and that allow the concrete realisation of the abstract principle. Take so-called "flexicurity", for instance, which for many States is the system that is supposed to take over from the old welfare model. It is in danger of becoming the phoenix of the third millennium. The only thing happening now is cuts in social benefits. There is no re-distribution of benefits among groups of the working population. With the crisis and the enormous resulting public deficits, welfare policies are entrusted to private, religious or non-religious bodies for their implementation, according to subsidiarity principles. The State is not even in a position to put the old offer of lower taxes on the negotiating table with citizens.

So even the old institutional pact has broken down. And we ask: what remains of what was once called the State?

2.5. Every self-employed worker in an unregulated profession, each one of us, might find the way reality has been portrayed here to be insufficient, or partial. For one thing, Italy has a very chequered history: the intense social conflict of the 1970s, for instance, contrasts with the sleepy social peace reigning in recent years. For another, the professional figures that have been created are the result of work flexibility and the Post-Fordist knowledge economy. We came into being during and as a result of the crisis of the "European social model", following a change in corporate management styles and principles. In the 1980s and 1990s, we benefited from robust market demand, with clients ready and willing to give us some space. We, the new arrivals, were treated almost hospitably. Had we not found favourable conditions, we would have found other ways of scraping by. So we have been knocked around like pinballs, yet we entered the market at one of the most incredible times of innovation. Many changes have not been negative, indeed many have been dynamic, offering greater opportunities to workers. Yet in one way or another, we have all been overwhelmed by the changes going on in the world and in production methods, and especially by the exceptional events of the second millennium. So, after coming into being when the "European social model" was already dying, we have an "uncertain" sense of citizenship. We have a strong sense of the public good but an unclear idea of the State, which we carry with us more as a family legacy than by virtue of ideological leanings. Neither do we have the ambition or the presumption of wishing to redefine it on our terms. We can but live this period of transition on a daily basis, deciding each day which actions and attitudes to take. One thing has changed for us, however. Let us say this clearly, once and for all: we want to be united, to be a single category. We want to stop acting individually. This is the only way to resume a negotiating position with the State that, although apparently dying out, will continue to exist in one form or another and to have a strong influence on the lives of worker-citizens. Being united is also the only way to retain a sense of the 'public good' and an awareness of what 'universal rights' are. We at ACTA have taken a step forward in this sense. Now we will explain, in brief, in which direction we intend to go, while attempting to fill in the blanks regarding the reality we now find ourselves in.

Part Three: About our vision of the alliance with other associations

When our Association, ACTA, was created in Milan, at the initiative of a small group of VAT-registered professionals, dozens of associations were already active in Italy with the declared aim of protecting professionals who are not obliged to join the Order of a professional Register in order to practise a profession. These are often new professional figures, coming into being with the evolution of technologies, production methods, changing lifestyles or professional services previously performed within companies or public administrations, the latter rendered necessary by outsourcing processes. In general terms, these professions offer "business services" provided to the vast media, creativity, events and the information universe, of which Milan is a leading centre, or in the sectors of training, healthcare, cultural assets and so on. The first impetus to form an association naturally comes with the need to recognise a single profession, with the definition of a profile or an identity marked by a specific competence. They are thus Associations that work more on distinctions than on similarities, on the distinctive traits of a competence rather than the common features uniting self-employed workers. ACTA has completely overturned this logic. It realises that the market has accepted the existence of these new professions and uses them extensively. There is a large void to fill, in the form of an organisation that tackles problems common to all professions not having their own Orders and some general problems faced by knowledge workers today, in particular problems faced by people practising a profession independently, without employment contracts and without an organised business structure, especially the problem of their fiscal relations with the State. The tax status of these workers is that of having a registered VAT (value added tax) number; thus they are authorised to issue an invoice, the only document allowed by law that they can use to seek monetary consideration for the services provided. ACTA therefore reaches out to all professions, shifting the focus from professional competence to the human and economic condition of the knowledge worker in the market. It is no coincidence that the inspiration for establishing a transversal Association for self-employed workers came from studies and researches that defined the parameters for an anthropology of self-employment. What does this mean? It has been proven that practising a profession as a salaried worker is very different from the situation of a self-employed worker in terms of mindset, perception of the world, attitude to remuneration and to the payer. In short, they are two very different experiences. The self-employed professional may therefore have a strong affinity with persons practising a very different profession from his own, while he may feel completely out of touch with the life of someone practising the same profession but as an employee. This shows that specific professional competence is not enough to bestow an identity on a person, and that Associations representing a single profession can only partially meet the needs of the worker-citizen. ACTA works on another level: it considers the legal-contractual form with which a professional activity is performed — and not the content of knowledge/skills — as being fundamental for relations established by the citizen. ACTA does not wish to reject the usefulness of professional Associations for the development of specialist skills and the constant upgrading of human capital. It totally rejects totalitarian and hegemonic tendencies, and accepts that a professional can be a member of more than one association.

By opening up to the human condition of the self-employed professional, ACTA seeks to anticipate changes in the collective perception, the swings in mood, mindset and habits, which often underlie the spirit of innovation or creativity much more than skill-perfecting exercises. Tacit innovation is what counts in the knowledge economy, the sort of innovation that can arise from a different way of looking at the world rather from a change in general market conditions.

3.1. So what is ACTA actually proposing, as a transversal organisation? Its programme can be summed up in five points: taxation and social security, universal rights, training, uniting to have more of a say, services to its members. With regard to the first point, taxation and social security, ACTA

a. denounces, with documentation to back up its claims, the current disparity of the self-employed worker as regards his taxation and social security situation compared with other worker-citizens

b. is pressuring the media to bring this situation to the attention of public opinion

c. is pressuring local and national politicians to improve, not worsen, relative laws and regulations

d. is promoting legislative initiatives and social policy measures to overcome this disparity or to improve the condition of VAT-registered professionals not protected by professional Orders

e. is demanding total transparency in the management of pension and benefit funds and information given to worker-citizens (e.g., by sending, annually, an up-to-date statement of payments made, the total amount of contributions paid in for pension purposes and projections on possible future pension sums)

f. is asking for support measures, such as the possibility of delaying social security payments with imputed contributions, such as the immediate deductibility of investments (with annual rather than longer term amortisation), and so on.

On the second point, universal rights, ACTA
a. is demanding:
– the right for VAT-registered professionals to receive personal assistance and protection in certain periods of their working life
– complete assistance in the event of sickness, including home-based care and parental leave
– a social safety net system in the event of a long-term lack of orders and state of unemployment
b. is seeking the adoption of a "universal maternity" measure, i.e. a sum to be paid for five months to all mothers, whether or not they are employees or self-employed, in permanent or temporary employment, working or not yet working; the maternity allowance should include the recognition of five months of

imputed contributions, to be calculated with reference to the period of greatest income based on one's entire working life, to be allocated to both parents.

On the third point, training, ACTA

a. is seeking the total deductibility of training-related costs

b. denounces the existing corporate training system and proposes the use of vouchers to be spent by workers for their training needs, possibly with a contribution made by workers and possibly outside the current accreditation system

c. is organising, by itself or in collaboration with other organisations, training courses and workshops, using cutting-edge communication technologies.

ACTA attaches great importance to the fourth point — uniting to have more of a say — and therefore

a. seeks to convince VAT-registered professionals of the need for them to come together in order to be heard and to try and improve their situation as regards relations with the State

b. is working to create a climate of real friendship, frank discussion and exchange of information among colleagues regarding the problems that they all encounter when practising their profession

c. is organising mobilisation initiatives, information materials and open protests in those cases in which misguided legislative initiatives pose dangers to the condition of VAT-registered professionals

d. proposes to other professional Associations the construction of permanent networks to work on common goals and interests, or the organisation of specific, temporary lobbying or training initiatives

e. joins international initiatives promoted by Associations of self-employed professionals and knowledge workers of other countries, which seek to make the voice of the category heard by European institutions

f. is opposed to any proposal that seeks to establish, for new professions, a system similar to that of the professional Orders.

The fifth point, services to its members, is closely tied up with the success of the alliance and with the resources that can be made available; currently ACTA

a. provides, via its website www.actainrete.it, a continuous flow of information on the social security and taxation situation of VAT-registered professionals and alerts on measures that bring changes to existing rules and procedures

b. has commenced training initiatives via local and distance learning courses

c. supports co-working initiatives aimed at its members

d. offers special agreements to its members for the subsidised purchase of work-related services (e.g., accountants, restaurant vouchers, etc.)

All activities performed by the Association are currently voluntary. This poses a serious limitation to the efficacy of ACTA's scope of actions. Elsewhere in

Europe and in the United States, similar Associations have a permanent staff, thanks to members' dues and donations from private Foundations. We can only hope that in Italy, too, there will be a growth in sensitivity regarding the ability of the alliance to carry more weight.

[In this section of the Manifesto, not included here, the fiscal and insurance conditions to which VAT holders are subject are described along with ACTA's specific proposals to improve them. To understand this section, the reader would have to know many technical aspects of Italian regulations, which even Italian freelancers, let alone an American reader, have difficulty understanding. For this reason, we have opted to save you the trouble.]

During the course of 2009 and in the first months of 2010, something new appeared on the horizon with regard to forms of representation of self-employment in Italy. Both trade unions (especially CGIL and CISL) and Craft Confederations set up internal bodies of representation aimed at the same base as that targeted by ACTA. Further to press campaigns, some political parties, perhaps in view of the imminent elections of April 2010, put forward proposals for a "self-employed workers' charter", presented at a regional level and intended for submission to Parliament. This sudden "awakening" of interest in professional self-employment can only be received favourably, partly as a sign that the work performed by ACTA has not been in vain. But we should add at once that, in view of how the initiative has been presented up until now, a serious danger lurks: trade unionists and politicians tend to identify more with the needs of public finance (on which they depend for their survival) than with the interests of the self-employed. In tandem with these new offers of representation, requests emerged for an increase in national insurance contributions from the self-employed. In some cases, they have been withdrawn thanks to the prompt action of ACTA and other Associations. In other cases, they have been suspended, like a threat hanging over the same interests they claim they want to protect. ACTA has had its say, having been explicitly invited to do so, about all of these initiatives, and has done so successfully, their ideas having been well received in most cases. It remains true, however, that improvements to the conditions of VAT-registered professionals largely depend on what they themselves are capable of doing. Our fate as worker-citizens is in our own hands — which are of course safer than anybody else's!

The recent state of the labour market and the devastating impact of the economic crisis have completely changed the lives of some categories of workers. Young professionals belonging to Orders (lawyers, architects, physicians, and so on) find themselves, both before and after graduating, and before and after the State qualifying examination, faced with the prospect of earning a pittance, so little as to make it impossible to pay in contributions to their pension funds, and with career prospects that are not encouraging, to say the least, or such as to force them to choose another trade. Young contract workers who have collaborated with public administrations and sometimes with private companies, which had the burden of paying in two-thirds of these workers' compulsory contributions to social security, are increasingly invited (and in some cases forced) to obtain a VAT number. This means they suddenly have to pass from a modest contribution rate to the 26.72% imposed on all self-employed professionals. ACTA opens its doors to both of these groups of workers, in the firm belief that it represents a valid point of reference not only for the problems of independent professional work but, more generally, the problems of knowledge work in a Post-Fordist age. Together we will succeed in having more of a say.

Milan, October 2010
Translation by Paul Warrington

ORGANIZING THE SELF-EMPLOYED:
A BATTLE FOR SOCIAL JUSTICE

A collection of essays edited and partially written by Andrea Fumagalli and me, with the title *Second Generation Independent Work. Scenes of Post-Fordism in Italy* was published by Feltrinelli (Milan) in 1997. The two main essays of the book, "Ten Parameters for Defining a Self-employed Workers Statute" and "For an Anthropology of Self-employed Workers" are presented here in the English translation by Paul Warrington.

That book deserves credit for opening a public debate for the first time in Italy on the figure of the independent — self-employed — worker, and particularly on unregulated professionals, which is to say those not belonging to traditional "liberal professions", such as doctors, lawyers, architects, journalists, etc. Four basic topics were presented in the book:

1. the world of independent work is in the process of changing fundamentally; the traditional figures of the farmer and shopkeeper are in decline while there is a rise in the so-called "knowledge workers" in the new professions or in services created by new life-styles

2. the independent worker is not an enterprise; they are people who earn their living with a business that requires an entrepreneurial spirit. Conceptually, an

enterprise is something else, a kind of organization with different roles carried out by different people

3. the independent worker has an autonomy whose limit lies in his or her dependence on a work relationship within which he or she is the weaker party

4. social security and welfare systems in industrialized countries are modeled on demand and the economic position of employees, excluding or safeguarding the independent worker only very peripherally.

These topics were collected with great diffidence and a certain hostility on the part of illustrious labor sociologists while arousing the interest of labor lawyers, who were much more prepared to discuss, without prejudice, the problems of the transformation of the world of work.

I believe that the reason for this sudden openness of labor lawyers was due to the deep analysis of the civil and labor law of independent work that is contained in the book by Adalberto Perulli, *Independent work. Work contract and intellectual professions*, published the year before, in 1996, by Giuffré Editore, which is still a milestone in labor law.

The seed was sown, and in the following years second generation independent workers began to become aware of their uniqueness and to create some sorts of representation. In 2004, ACTA was founded and began to work systematically to clarify the actual living and working conditions of unregulated independent professionals. ACTA represents something new because it wants to be an across-the-board organization, in contrast with the associations that had existed up to then, which were rigidly subdivided by profession. Representation of regulated and non regulated independent work was conducted by professional associations united under one or more umbrella organisations. ACTA was not one of these because ACTA did not want to represent one or more professions: ACTA wanted to represent a *professional condition*.

However, the cultural and political environment continued to be hostile, particularly the environment influenced by the ideologies of the left and the trade union movement, which were unable to conceive a world of work different from that of employees. They considered non standard, precarious work as transitional work waiting to become dependent, independent work as a disguised form of dependent work. No doubt, a part of second generation independent work is a disguised form of dependent work — such as those who work for platform capitalism (Uber, Deliveroo, etc.). Furthermore, the widespread public opinion was that independent workers were tax evaders. There was undoubtedly some truth to this rumor, but again in this case, ACTA succeeded in clarifying the situation. ACTA demonstrated that while it is easy for a professional to avoid paying taxes when they work for an individual, it is impossible when they work for a company or public administration, since they are a cost to these entities and, as such, it is necessary, as well as in the company's interest, for their work to be documented.

Public opinion was therefore disconcerted when ACTA successfully demonstrated that the tax burden of second generation independent workers, who are obliged to pay social security contributions, is equal to or larger than that of employees. In the following years, this became the argument upon which ACTA decided to concentrate its efforts and which it carried forward in total isolation.

But the times were changing. International experiences and contacts established in Europe and the US provided strong support to ACTA activities. The example of the Freelancers Union was an inspiration and teacher. A special affinity formed immediately, and ACTA was made a *sister organization*.

At the same time, Europe was setting up a network of independent work associations (EFIP, the European Forum of Independent Professionals), which ACTA joined right away, providing support that was recognised by its Vice-President being named EFIP Vice-President. So, using the language of the Third International ironically, you could say that ACTA was "marching alongside" the great international freelance movement, which has now also caught the interest of academic research.

What triggered this movement? One fundamental factor was the 2008 financial crisis, which began a stagnant period in the world economy, particularly in Europe, and brutally brought to light the discomfort, fragmentation and frustration of a middle class in which independent work is an essential component.

Many professionals suddenly went from a standard middle-class life to poverty conditions; new entries found a sluggish market paying less and less (and often paying them later and later or not paying them at all). The past aura of success surrounding freelancers, making them the symbolic figures of winners in the neo-liberal era, disappeared miserably, and "knowledge workers" discovered that they needed safeguarding, needed to overcome their "selfish individualism", needed to associate themselves, needed to find new forms of self help.

This realization was not immediate. At first, in 2008, -09, -10 and -11, generations that had never experienced an economic crisis, who had no memory of it, clung to the illusion that it was a passing, cyclical crisis. In 2013, -14, things changed, also because politics recognized that society had come to a boiling point, and the old parties were ousted by new movements that, in a very short time and with no historical background, conquered in some European countries vast slices of the electorate and in Italy too.

The crisis strongly affected employment, removing many certainties from employed work, throwing young people standing at the edge of the work market into the cruel ghetto of prolonged precariousness and clearly demonstrating the inadequacy of a welfare system built after the Second World War in a world of production that was now a thing of the past.

And finally ACTA came out of isolation, particularly due to the efforts and competence of its president, Anna Soru, not only becoming a social partner of the political class and of the government, to whom ACTA presents the demands of second generation independent workers, but also succeeding in bringing other independent work associations onto its platform, even those close to trade union organizations.

Thus, a sufficiently united, even if not homogeneous, front of independent work has been created that has obtained credibility with the institutions and has successfully achieved two consistent legislative results: a reduction in public social security contributions, and the Statute of Independent Work approved in May 2017 by Parliament.

But, as we know, crisis years are also years of deep transformation and innovation, and capitalism has always known how to show unexpected vitality in these two areas. From the crucible of crisis is born the world of tomorrow. From the reduction in available resources are born the grass roots idea of a sharing economy with a strong element of self help and cooperation. Capitalism immediately appropriates them, managing to carve out new frontiers of work flexibility, a new business model, in which the work performer, the worker, provides his or her energy, his or her human capital, but especially provides his or her heritage of assets.

What is called "capitalism of digital platforms" is a far-reaching phenomenon which — and here my professional experience assists me — has interested the world of production and distribution in logistical organisation. Before Uber or Airbnb or Deliveroo there was Amazon, which revolutionised the world of logistics through home delivery, thanks to the power of its digital platform.

The characteristic of platform capitalism is its ambiguous but always seductive call to the autonomy of work. Self-employment becomes a promise.

So the spectre of "false independent work" inexorably returns, after we hoped to have exorcized it once and for all. So the risk – also for labor lawyers – is to fall back into the sterile discussion of how to distinguish "real", "authentic" independence from "false", while their attention would be better turned to bottom up transformations and innovations.

The crisis has stimulated new ideas not only for capitalism but also for those who are paying a high price for it. In the world of independent work, intermittent work, new technical professions, and old and new creative professions, the idea and practice of mutualism are making more and more inroads. An example of great interest is the *Société Mutuelle des Artistes,* SMart, with its headquarters in Brussels, which is active in nine European countries and has tens of thousands of members.

But there is something else new. All those who are closely following the activities of independent work associations will have noticed that recently, with the continuing crisis and after focusing their attention on the issues of social security and welfare, they are now making the problem of work payment a priority: late payments or missing payments, races to the lowest bids (particularly in public administration), in a word, the focus is now the problem of income. It is a way to underline the drama of inequalities, to return to the center of western society the class that constitutes its backbone, the middle class. In fact, in October 2016, New York City passed the first ever law that lays out the terms for payments and contracts between businesses and freelancers, the "Freelance Isn't Free Act" (FIFA).

As a final remark, I would like to express my gratitude and great appreciation to our labor lawyer friends who have not left us alone in these years, who have done their best to accompany our efforts by noting innovations taking place in society, being stimulated by them to transform legal thinking and make regulations more flexible, more responsive to society's needs. It has been a significant contribution to the modernization of our society. This does not mean at all that views were completely the same or that there was a confusion over roles, but simply an open, intense dialogue that has changed things in both politics and public opinion.

Translation by Kristy Lynn Davis